The Blackpool Rock

The Blackpool Rock

Guns, Gangs and Door Wars
In Britain's Wildest Town

Stephen Sinclair

MILO BOOKS LTD

Published in July 2008 by Milo Books

ISBN 978 1 903854 80 8

Typeset by Jayne Walsh

Printed in Great Britain by
CPD Wales, Blaina

MILO BOOKS LTD
The Old Weighbridge
Station Road
Wrea Green
Lancs PR4 2PH
United Kingdom
www.milobooks.com

About the Author

Date of birth: 13 August 1957.
Place: Ashton-under-Lyne, Manchester.

At six feet and two inches in height and weighing in at seventeen and a half stone, I stand out in a crowd. But through good luck – or a bit of friendly persuasion – I have only ever been found guilty of one criminal offence, which was for actual bodily harm when I was eighteen years of age. That is not bad when you consider how long I have been working on the doors.

Over the years I have had lumps knocked, bitten and cut out of me. I have been shot at and shot back. I have been involved in hundreds of violent encounters that I have not even been questioned about, let alone been charged with, so I have to be careful what I say and how I write my story that I don't drop myself or any of my friends in it. I have changed the names of some characters in this book. This is to protect guilty parties that have not been prosecuted. The innocent are okay and can look after themselves.

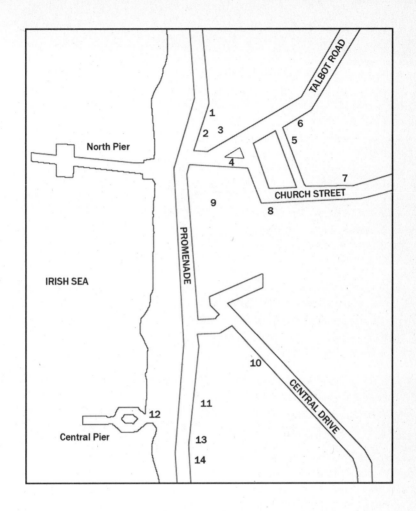

BLACKPOOL PUBS AND CLUBS MENTIONED

1. Shaboo
2. The Business
3. Bunters
4. Addisons
5. Secrets
6. Just Ji's
7. The Syndicate
8. Winter Gardens
9. Promises
10. The Village
11. The Adam and Eve
12. The Dixieland/Oz
13. Lips
14. The Foxhall
15. Mecca Ballroom

Contents

Prologue

I WAS MANAGING to block most of the punches being thrown at me. Luckily for me, the gang I was fighting were getting in each other's way. I dropped one of the bastards with a big right and took the opportunity to get through the opening and find some space.

I knew I was hurt; all my strength was leaving me but I couldn't understand why. There was no pain and I hadn't taken any big shots to my head, even though I had been surrounded by about eight of the twats all trying to do their worst.

Two of them were coming at me now, both big bastards. I pushed myself upright from the shop front to meet them face-on, but I had nothing left. A figure flew past me from behind, smashing into my would-be assailants and taking them away from me. Other people came running across the street from the club entrance.

'Steve! Steve! Are you okay mate? You're bleeding all over the place.'

Lifting my suit jacket, I saw blood spurting from beneath my ribcage. My left trouser leg was already soaked red. I was losing life and I was losing it fast.

Well if this was going to be my final battle, I wasn't going to go without a fight …

1

Busting the Bullies

AUGUST 13, 1957, was a great date for me but not so good for some of England's police forces. I was born the youngest of three children to Iris and Joe Sinclair. My brother Colin was five years older than me and my sister Lorraine was three years older. We lived in a terraced house on Catherine Street, just off the main Oldham Road in Ashton-under-Lyne. It was then in Lancashire but is now Greater Manchester.

At that time, my old man, Joe, ran a scrap metal yard. He was also quite a well-known villain, having served time at Her Majesty's finest accommodation for offences such as armed robbery and GBH. My dad was not a big man, he stood five feet ten inches and weighed about eleven stone, but he was immensely strong, no doubt from all the heavy lifting in the scrap yard – and possibly the odd safe or two. He loved spending time with us. He had a great sense of humour and enjoyed making us laugh with stories from his past.

My favourite one was how during World War Two, the lorry he was travelling in through France broke down in the countryside. As the youngest member of his platoon, he was left to guard it. The next morning was very foggy and my dad, who had been sleeping under the vehicle, heard someone walking towards the lorry. All he could see through the fog were a pair of polished jackboots marching towards him, so being young and inexperienced, instead of challenging, 'Who goes there?' he just shot about three feet above the top of the boots. The figure dropped like a stone and fell into a ditch at the side of the road. Hours later, when his platoon leader returned with some towing gear, my dad was still under the truck with his rifle aimed down the road.

'What you doing under there, you daft sod?' shouted the platoon leader. 'Did that French gendarme not come out to see you this morning?'

My father gave me some great advice, which I have endeavoured to follow to the best of my ability: 'Never plead guilty son, things can change,' and, 'Always be nice in the first instance; you can always turn aggressive if you have to, but if you start aggressive it's too late to be nice.' He also told me never to be afraid to apologise if I was in the wrong.

My mother was not a very big lady; in fact she stood only five feet two inches tall (makes me wonder where I came into the equation) but she was very strong-willed and she gave my father an ultimatum. If he went back inside again, we would not be there when he got out. It was that simple. It was just after this ultimatum that I was taken seriously ill with pneumonia. Before I was two years old, I had suffered from this illness three times. The doctors informed my parents that I might not survive; they said the best thing for me was the sea air. My family decided they would have to move. But where to?

Blackpool was not far away but it was one of my dad's old stomping grounds and my mother feared that he might be tempted to slip back into his old ways. My grandparents on my dad's side had recently retired to Hayling Island, near Portsmouth, on the south coast. After visiting the area, it was decided that the family would head south and that's how Portsmouth Football Club gained another supporter.

The area we moved to, Southsea, was definitely more

upmarket than Ashton-under-Lyne but growing up in Portsmouth with a Manchester accent managed to get all three of us kids into a few scraps. Colin, despite being the oldest, could not fight to save his life. He came home from school many times minus such things as his school tie, his cap and even his spectacles. One time he came home with tyre marks across his chest where someone had run him over with their push bike. Lorraine, however, could fight like a Rottweiler and was always scrapping with other kids, both girls and boys.

On one occasion, I was still at Albert Road junior school in Southsea while Lorraine and Colin had both moved up into grammar school, having passed their eleven-plus exams (no pressure on me, eh!). Lorraine came home from school and asked me if I wanted to go to the local park with her. I was about ten years old and had recovered my health. When we arrived at the park, a crowd of girls was waiting for my sister. She explained that another girl had picked a fight with her earlier that day at her school and they had arranged to meet here and settle it. Lorraine passed me a rounders bat that she had brought with her and made me promise that if anyone else joined in, I would hit them with it. I asked her what I should do if she was getting beat up. I can still remember the dirty look she gave me when she told me not to be so fucking stupid. Of course, she won.

It was around this time I had my run-in with the supposed cock of the school. His name was Gary Howarth and I thought we were good pals, but chemistry and male hormones were changing all of us. I can't remember the girl's name – what else would it have been over? – but we squared up to each other outside the school gates, which were less than fifty yards from where we lived on Napier Road. Bam! My nose was squashed before I even saw him swing. My eyes began to water and I heard someone yell, 'He's crying, do him Gary.' The next thing I knew a teacher was pulling me off of him. I had thrown him over some dustbins, dived on top of him and pummelled him with both hands.

The best thing after the teacher stopped the fight was the look of horror on the faces of all those who had supported Gary and not me. I grinned at my pals as I was hauled off to the headmaster's office and he was taken to the school nurse. Next morning, Gary and his battered face and me and my squashed nose (I can still press it flat now) came face to face again in the head's office. True to form for young lads from all over the world, we remained friends and the girl got the push. I had also learned a valuable lesson: I could have a row.

My mum, God bless her, despite her small stature had steel in her veins and a temper to match. Many a time when we were naughty she would chase us around the house until she caught us and gave us a wallop. One day she realised she was having less effect than usual when I started laughing, so she went out and bought a riding crop because she was fed up of hurting her hand when she hit any of us. This had the desired effect and soon had me locking myself in the bathroom until my dad got home.

As a kid I always looked forward to my dad getting home from work. He would save me a half a sandwich, curled up at the edges by the end of the day, and some tea in his flask, nearly cold but it tasted wonderful. This made me feel special because neither my brother nor sister got any; remember I was the youngest.

My eleven-plus exam came and went, with the result that I got into Havant Grammar School, near to Emsworth, approximately eleven miles outside of Portsmouth where we had just relocated. I would have got some stick from my brother and sister if I had failed. I can't say a lot about Havant Grammar School because I was not there long. I was expelled for fighting. Talk about stuck-up twats with no sense of humour! Anyway the local education authority offered me a place at St John's

College, where students had to wear straw boater hats as part of their uniform, or Warblington Secondary School, where a lot of my friends already suffered. Guess which one I chose. My mother in her wisdom decided not to buy me the new school uniform but to make me wear my Havant Grammar School blazer and tie. With hindsight this was not the best decision a mother could make for her youngest son who had just been expelled from another school for continually fighting. I was involved in three separate fights on my first day.

As young teenagers we were always aware of girls, but when we first sampled their delights our whole outlook on life changed. All life seemed to consist of for quite some time was shagging and fighting, not necessarily in that order. School went to the back of the queue. I lost my virginity to the sister of one of my friends in the local village graveyard, at least I think it was her; it was pitch black, freezing cold and she moaned a lot, so it might have been one of the cemetery's residents.

My school years passed by with plenty of visits to the headmaster to receive six of the best. For those of you too young to know, six of the best was administered across your buttocks with a thin bamboo cane, often leaving you too sore to sit when you went back to your classroom. Although I had passed my eleven-plus I was not academic at all, in fact I hated school. I was thrown out of French lessons within a week of being at Warblington. I still hate the French to this day. The teacher, a Mr Michelle, came from Algiers and we did not hit it off right from the start of my first lesson. Things got worse from then on.

Sport was my saving grace at school. I made nearly all the teams available except for the swimming team, as I still had difficulties with my chest from my bouts of pneumonia when I was younger. I can honestly say I was also popular with my classmates and peers, but bullying at school was rife then. Some older lads kept having a chip at me and my friends, always team-handed, led by a guy called Johnny Cutler.

I was at the Warblington School youth club, when Trevor Locke, one of this older group who picked on me and some of my friends all the time, said something he thought was clever or funny about me. What he didn't realise was that I was not scared of him, especially when he was not with his gang but with some girls from my year that he was trying to impress. I turned round and belted him. This escalated into a scuffle that I managed to come out of on top.

Next day it was the talk of the school and all my pals were made up, but I knew that Johnny Cutler and his friends wouldn't be happy with me. I kept getting the angry looks and snide comments from Cutler, though Trevor Locke looked a bit sheepish. I knew payback was going to come sooner or later but there was nothing I could do about it except try to stay in public places as much as possible. All the euphoria I had felt the previous evening in beating Locke had now deserted me. It is the waiting that I don't like; the longer it takes to happen, the worse it is.

They finally collared me at lunchtime in one of the stairwells next to Class 4C. Now 4C were the same year as me but they were leaving at Easter. These were the kids who hated school and always rebelled against the teachers, and they had already reached the age of fifteen, the minimum leaving age at that time. A lot of the lads in this class were my mates, so in no time there was a group of us and a group of them. This was a different game, and they were not so keen on these odds. Someone came up with the idea of Locke and me having a one-on-one. He couldn't back down and I definitely wouldn't.

Once everyone had formed a circle, Locke charged straight at me. He ran onto a right hand that took his feet level with my shoulders. Crunch! His head hit a doorstop and he went out like a light, with blood pouring everywhere.

After the ambulance had been and gone, taking the headbanger away to hospital, the headmaster must have finally got the information he was after, because I was summoned to his office. Mr Rankin was a big man and he was very heavy-handed with the cane when dishing out our punishment. I was very nervous when I entered his office and became even more so when I was confronted by a uniformed police officer. The end result was a week's suspension – more like a reward than a punishment – from school and a telling off from the Old Bill. My mum and dad were a bit upset but when they heard the full story, they were sweet.

I managed to get hold of another of the bullying gang, David Sparrowhawke, at the local park in Emsworth. Once I had attracted his attention, he quickly denounced his friends, claiming, 'They made me do it.' This took a lot of the enjoyment out of giving him a slap, but not all of it. And I never did get even with Johnny Cutler.

I left school in July when we broke up for the summer holidays, three weeks before my fifteenth birthday. I had sat no O-levels nor achieved any qualifications, but I just wanted out of school. My mum and dad were not well off and the only real holidays we had as children were in sunny Blackpool. I had never been abroad, so I made up my mind and, with my parents' consent, I joined the Merchant Navy, still at the age of fifteen.

I enrolled for three months at the National Sea Training College in Gravesend, Kent. It was a residential course, and when I returned home from college for the first time, my family were surprised at the change in my appearance. After long hours of rowing lifeboats on the River Thames, my physique had bulked up; I was now six feet and one inch tall and weighed in at about twelve stone.

My first ship was the *Queen Elizabeth 2*, the famous Cunard ocean liner, sailing from Southampton, the home of Portsmouth's FC's local football rivals. Pompey fans like myself hated them with a passion, although I don't know why, as all the ones I met were okay. Mind you, if I had met them on the terraces it might have been different. As a junior rating I worked on board the ship a total of three months on and one month off. I soon discovered the ship was called 'Queen' Elizabeth for a reason; it was full of them. The officer in charge of the junior ratings was the food and beverage manager, Gordon Phillips. He was a three-striper, answerable only to the hotel manager and the ship's captain, and he was one mean queen with attitude. He also looked after his own.

All the junior ratings were boys under the age of eighteen but I was the youngest, still only fifteen. As with any institution, there was a pecking order on board, especially amongst the junior ratings. After one or two altercations with a couple of my new shipmates, I was as close to the top of this order as I needed to be to make my life easier for the foreseeable future.

One thing we could not stand or tolerate was a thief, and when we found one, we took action. We placed his hand in one of the door frames and then closed the door on it.

This led to me leaving the *QE2* for a time before a full investigation was launched. I tried another shipping company, P&O, and signed on the cruise ship *Oriana*, but after a run-in with the chief steward I was soon heading shore side, back home to Emsworth – and more trouble.

2

Pompey Boot Boy

MILLWALL WERE COMING. That was all we kept
hearing for what seemed like months, but was in reality
probably only a few days. There was no organised football
hooliganism in the early Seventies as there is today, no
internet or mobile phones available for arranging meetings, just land lines and word of mouth. But Millwall had
one of the most feared crews in the country, bar none,
and everyone in Pompey knew they were coming.

By the age of fifteen I had been following Portsmouth
FC for a good few years. I first went to games with my
dad and his pal but as I grew older I started to go to
the ground with my own mates, Mark Wood and Peter
Juggins. Mark, who I had met when I first moved to
Portsmouth at two years of age, was ten days older than
me and had a very dark complexion. We called him the
'Little Jap' because he was bang into his martial arts and
achieved black belt status. Pete was four or five months
older than us and I met him when I moved to Emsworth,
just before my eleventh birthday. Both remain my good
friends to this day.

During this era, the fashion for youths of my age was
dominated by the skinhead look: short or no hair and
big fuck-off Doc Marten boots, hence the name Pompey
Boot Boys. Suedeheads were also just starting to make
an appearance, with crombie coats, interlaced loafers and

sta-press trousers, but they were mainly the older lads who could get into night clubs and wanted to look smart.

I had fought plenty of fights throughout my school days, even gang fights with boys from other schools, but I will never forget the buzz that went through me that first time on the Fratton End Terrace. People who have not been there cannot understand how the individual mentality becomes part of a mob mentality. It even happens to trained police officers; you will often see two or three riot police armed with batons attacking single unarmed football fans or protesters on news programmes. Remember the miners' strike? Every decent-sized team in those days had its hooligans, and the two main aims were taking ends and taking scarves. Pompey was a tough city with tough fans, but even we met our match on occasion.

Before the much-anticipated Millwall match, one of the older Pompey lads, who worked for British Rail, found an internal memo meant for the local constabulary giving the estimated time for a football special arriving at Fratton from Waterloo Station in London. It would come in at approximately 1.30pm on the Saturday afternoon. It even had the number of carriages: twelve. Twelve carriages full of Millwall, fuck me.

Pete and I both lived in Emsworth and had to get the train down to Fratton. We would always meet up with a lad called Fred who travelled down from Chichester. Chichester is halfway between Portsmouth and Brighton and Fred's mates supported Brighton (wankers). Fred had better taste: he was a top man was Fred, always up for it.

One of the stops on the way to Portsmouth is Havant, and at Havant there was always a group of other lads from Leigh Park who we met up with. They were all of a similar age to ourselves and all wore the same fashion: jeans, sta-press trousers and big cherry-red boots. We would call at my mate Mark's house on Francis Avenue, about half a mile from Fratton Park, at about eleven o'clock on the morning of the match, just as the pubs were opening. At fifteen we could get served in some pubs but not all of them near the ground. We used Mark's house phone to arrange to meet some other lads on Goldsmith Avenue, near Fratton railway station. There was a pub there where you could watch the trains pull in to the platform.

We waited impatiently, along with about a hundred other young Portsmouth fans all dressed the same: Harrington jackets in various colours, mine being red, Fred Perry or Ben Sherman shirts, faded rolled-up jeans with braces and shiny, high-laced Doc Marten boots. Our average age would have been about seventeen and we were all full of ourselves.

Then the Millwall train pulled in.

We all crossed the road to the wall and railings cutting us off from railway property. As the train doors opened, we raised our hands and cheered.

'Portsmouth! Portsmouth!'

The reply was instantaneous, and thunderous.

'MILLWALL! MILLWALL!'

Their fans poured onto the platform. What the fuck! There were two trains, not one. All of us Pompey lads looked at each other in horror; these weren't kids, they were geezers, and big, hard-looking geezers at that. It suddenly dawned on us: this was the route to the ground from the station and we were in-between, with no main Portsmouth firm in sight. Fuck that. It was time for a tactical withdrawal.

'What's that mean?' shouted one of our not-so-clued-up mob.

'Run like fuck,' I replied.

And we did.

Later I stood in the Fratton End with the main bulk of the Pompey crew, made up of smaller groups from different areas in and around Portsmouth, exactly like our little crew from Emsworth, Leigh Park, Havant and Hayling Island. We faced the turnstiles where the Millwall fans were due to approach and enter the ground. We could see down the length of Frogmore Road that leads to the Fratton End. The atmosphere around us was electric.

Portsmouth is a naval dockyard city with plenty of big, rough men, but the majority of our crew were in their late teens. What we had seen of the Millwall firm made us realise the age difference. Everyone was on edge. I could see the fear on their faces and mine was probably a mirror image. The older faces on the Portsmouth firm, names like Ginger Howard – who looks just like the psycho gangster out of the film *Snatch* – were shouting for us to stand as Millwall fans poured through the turnstiles. Where were the police when you needed them?

I would like to say, in the words of Winston Churchill, that it was long, it was hard and it was cruel – but it wasn't. They attacked our end from the front, with hundreds of their fans cramming the stairways while their main force ran through the walkway under the terrace and outflanked us. They hit us from behind before we even knew they were there. I think it may have been the first time that the Fratton End had been taken, certainly since I had become a teenager and realised that match day was not just about watching the game.

After a frightening but exciting match, in which we adopted guerrilla tactics of hit-and-run – hit as hard as you can and then run as fast as you can back to the safety of your own crew – I found myself as a guest of the local constabulary, along with a lot of other Portsmouth lads. As a rule at that time, the police would just eject you from the ground if the offence was not too serious and leave you to your own devices. If the turnstiles were still open you could just pay another two shillings and sixpence, or whatever the price was, and go back in.

I did just that and was involved in a fight near the toilets when the same copper who had just thrown me out collared me again. The police were quite busy that day, as you can imagine. Though I was only fifteen I looked older and this time the police left me in a cell until after 11pm, considerate bastards that they are. When I asked them for the phone call to which I was entitled, saying, 'I need to let my mum know where I am because she'll be worried about me,' they laughed.

'Big, hard hooligan got to let his mummy know where he is,' sneered one of them. Piss-taking bastards. They soon stopped laughing when I told them I was only fifteen.

By the time my mum and dad turned up at Southsea police station – the Millwall fans would have gone to Eastney or Northend nick – at just past midnight, I was drinking tea and eating biscuits and the Inspector in charge could not apologise enough.

'What do you think you are doing, keeping my son here until this time without informing us?' my mother, who was clearly not amused, asked the Inspector.

'He wouldn't even tell us his name, let alone how old he is,' replied the Inspector indignantly. 'There are no charges, he is free to go. As long as you leave now,' he added, with a bit more force.

My mum was still angry at me and the police but my old man ruffled my hair and gave me a crafty wink and a smile.

One of the most memorable matches was away at Charlton Athletic in the FA Cup. All the Sunday papers the next day had pictures of Portsmouth fans on their front pages. 'Blue and white pilgrimage,' read one headline. If I remember rightly it was the fourth or fifth round and we had not been that well placed for years. Fourteen thousand away fans, don't forget we weren't a First Division team, fourteen thousand, fucking magic.

There were pictures of coaches, cars, vans, even motorbikes driving through the streets of London, all with blue and white Portsmouth scarves blowing in the wind. Then there were the football special trains. I travelled up to Charlton by coach with the regular group of lads from Emsworth and Leigh Park who all used to drink in the Star public house in Havant. The police would be all over the fans on the trains, stopping them from drinking alcohol and even searching them, but it did not dampen our spirits. Charlton's crew didn't put up much of a show that day, probably because of our numbers. Their team did rather better on the pitch, but a late finish gave our lads a great win.

The Valley, Charlton's ground, was not too far from Millwall's Den, and, Millwall fans being what they are, they must have fancied a row. I'm not sure who they were playing that day but their rivals obviously did not bring a firm because instead they decided to target us. A few of us left the ground before the end of the match to see if we could find any of the Charlton crew, a tactic that had worked well for us in the past. A couple of the younger lads who we used as spotters scurried off up the street to see what they could find. Two minutes later, they ran back around the corner like they were being chased by some demons from hell.

'Fucking Millwall,' they screamed. 'They're right behind us.'

There was not that many of us but those that were there all ran to the corner of the street from which the young Pompey lads had appeared. We pulled up fast when we got there. Fuck! There were hundreds of them, all walking down the street towards us. They were spread across the width of the road and all had big daft grins on their faces, obviously thinking we would run away.

Looking at them, I thought to myself these weren't the geezers that we would normally see arriving at Fratton Park; these were young lads just like us. A huge roar came from the Charlton ground. Portsmouth had won with a late goal.

'Fucking yes, let's have it!'

Their big daft grins disappeared as we laid into them, feet and fists flying. In truth we would have ended up getting well and truly battered, but at that moment the main crew of our boys turned the corner. Hundreds of Pompey lads went home from Charlton wearing Millwall scarves. What a result.

Sometimes we came unstuck and we were on the receiving end but that is what it was all about. You were with a crew of lads travelling to someone else's turf. In ancient times it would have been with swords and spears and we would have been raping and pillaging or stealing livestock and young women.

Manchester United at home was an evening kick-off. Obviously the long haul to the south coast was not highly rated on United supporters' fixture lists, but the Red Devils always brought some fans. One of these was outside the ground shouting the odds. He had United scarves tied around both wrists and hanging from his belt. He had backed a few Pompey lads off already before I decided to tackle him. I jumped into him, butting with my head then punching with lefts and rights. He was taller than me with a big feathered haircut that would have been considered stylish in that day and age. I managed to put him down then went in to introduce him to Dr Marten.

All of a sudden I was yanked backwards and saw two big suits. They were CID.

'You're nicked, son,' growled the one that twisted my arm up my back.

Now these two coppers were both bigger and heavier than me and they led me over to a Mini and threw me in the back. Then they squeezed themselves into the front, started the car and set off.

'So you like a fight do you?' asked the gorilla in the passenger seat, looking back at me. 'Well; you've got a choice now,' he said, smiling. 'A good hiding from us or down to the police station and we'll charge you.'

It only took me a second to make a decision: 'A good hiding from you.' Bollocks, what else would I do?

They pulled into a deserted business park not that far from the football ground and both of them got out. I climbed out from the back of the Mini, no easy task in itself, wondering if I could outrun them. I stood there waiting. Okay, I was bricking it, thinking, what are you waiting for.

'Good lad,' said the gorilla that had offered me the option, then they both got back in the Mini and drove off; leaving me bemused but very grateful.

Whenever Pompey played too far away to travel, at places like Grimsby, we would jump on a train and go to Southampton or Brighton, whoever was playing at home. Sometimes there could be as many as thirty of us. On one such occasion, Southampton were playing at home against Chelsea. About twenty of us disembarked at Southampton station only to see a fair crew of lads already milling about just outside. We thought they were scummers (Southampton fans) waiting for Chelsea fans but then saw they were wearing blue and white scarves. They obviously thought we were scummers and they prepared themselves for some trouble. They could not believe it when the 'Portsmouth!' chant rang out from our little firm. Once they found out why we were there, they were only too happy to join up with us.

We went into a pub called The Bargate in Southampton city centre and were having a good drink when a load of Southampton fans came in. Within a minute the Chelsea fans had gone. One of the scummers came over to us and said, 'You Chelsea cunts had better fuck off with the rest of your mates.'

We looked at him and laughed.

'We aren't Chelsea, you wanker,' I told him. 'We are Portsmouth.'

Then we went for them, grabbing chairs, glasses and anything else we could get hold of. We went through them like a dose of salts and then legged it before the police arrived.

Once we were inside The Dell, Southampton's ground, we joined up with some more Chelsea fans and made our way into the home end. In no time at all we were in the middle of it, surrounded by scummers and battling like mad just to survive. Finally we were also surrounded by police officers, who escorted us out of the home end. The Chelsea fans started cheering and singing, 'Portsmouth, Portsmouth.' What a buzz that was.

On one trip, instead of going by train, Mark turned up at my house on a big Kawasaki motorbike. Mark was into his bikes. 'Jump on, Steve,' he said with a big grin. As we neared Southampton we passed a motorbike cop going in the opposite direction. He seemed to take a lot of interest in us. Sure enough, he indicated to turn and followed us. I was nearly thrown off the bike as Mark accelerated like a lunatic.

'What are you doing, you nutter?' I shouted in his ear.

'Sorry Steve, I should have told you. The bike's stolen. Hold on mate.'

We never made it to the game but we didn't get caught either.

Another time with Mark we were in Southampton again. We had just left their ground when we were confronted by a small group of scummers blocking our path. Knowing that bluffing our way past them would be difficult, we just flew straight in to them shouting, 'Portsmouth!' The surprise of our attack scattered them and we were through them, running down the street and around a corner. When we stopped, Mark collapsed and started to be sick. He had taken a kick to his balls and with the adrenalin rush at the time he had not felt it, but as soon as we stopped he suffered a delayed reaction.

A police car that was passing pulled up. Mark was on the floor and had gone a bit green around the gills. After I had explained how we had been jumped, the police were great and radioed for an ambulance to attend. They even stayed with us until it arrived for which we were very grateful, what with angry scummers still prowling around.

I waited patiently in the A&E department and after a while Mark appeared, looking quite embarrassed. When I asked him what was wrong, he explained. He had been stretchered in to the hospital and after some time he was examined by an attractive female doctor. When she started the examination, Mark's pain must have subsided and nature progressed. In plain English, Mark got an erection and subsequently he was asked to leave.

Although I really enjoyed the buzz of football violence and I can see how some people become addicted to it, for me enough was enough. Sooner or later I was going to end up getting nicked and staying nicked. As we got a bit older, we graduated to discos and nightclubs instead of just one or two pubs, and with us having transport this gave us access to loads of young females – and a lot more scrapping along the entire south coast.

3

Fighting Mad

JOANNA'S BAR WAS a disco on Southsea seafront that we used on a regular basis. It was also frequented by lads who served in the Royal Navy, which meant things could get a bit lively in there, but the doormen were good guys who we knew from Portsmouth football matches. It was also always full of girls that were up for it.

One weekend I was in the club with Pete Juggins and Mark Wood when there was a big kick-off. The doormen were outnumbered and under a bit of pressure, so we waded in to help them. This led to Rick, the head doorman, asking if I fancied helping them out if they were ever short. I found this quite funny, with me probably being the youngest person in the club. I believe Joanna's Bar is still there today and by all accounts still has plenty of trouble.

A good lad that Pete and I were at school with, called Dave Hayward, joined our little gang. This brought us up to a nice even number of four. Although we were in the same year as each other at school, Dave was eleven months older than me and had already passed his driving test. He was the proud owner of a Ford Capri that he loved more than girls and, boy, did Dave love the girls.

Although he was an apprentice bricklayer Dave was not your typical builder type. He was a good-looking lad who liked to keep himself fit and he also liked to keep up with fashion. I remember him as being the first lad to have a feather cut in or around our area. I would not say that Dave was vain but you could spoil his night by telling him his hair was out of place or that he had a spot coming up on his face. All said and done, he enjoyed a good fight and he was very useful. We became the best of buddies and were inseparable for a couple of years.

Now that we had access to a car, the south coast was our playground, places like Hayling Island and Bognor Regis and anywhere in between. The clubs on Hayling Island provided us with a lot of entertainment, places like the Beach club and the Solent club. Trouble was never far away.

One incident came at a nightclub called the Red Knight. This was on Hayling Island, in a holiday camp named The Sinah. Warren, Dave, Pete, Mark and I had gone there on a Christmas Eve, the place was rammed and everyone was having a good time. However, a group of local lads knew we were from Emsworth and decided to start giving us a hard time, along with the big stare. There were quite a few more of them than us but that had never bothered me before and it wasn't going to bother me now.

Pete or Mark came back from the toilet and said he had been threatened: either we leave now or we would get a good kicking. I looked over at these lads leaning against the bar, smirking at us, thinking that we had no choice but to leave. There was one of them about my size who thought he was the bee's knees. He was starting to piss me off. I looked at Dave, Pete and Mark. They knew what I was thinking and they all nodded.

We would have had to walk past these cunts to get out of the club anyway, so they weren't too worried when we all turned and started walking towards them. The one I didn't like straightened up a bit with that daft smirk on his face.

Surprise!

I jumped in and kicked him straight under his chin. He flew backwards over the bar. That was it; we were into them then like foxes into a hen house. The security came running inside but they were not doormen as such, more like Group 4 with daft uniforms on. They had no chance of controlling the situation so they called the police, who came and shut the place early. Merry fucking Christmas. The club ended up being closed through the New Year celebrations too.

We continued to go to Hayling Island for many months after, up until I left Emsworth, and even then we would go there if I was visiting the area. We also started travelling to places like Southampton, Bournemouth or Brighton at weekends because we were getting barred from a lot of the local venues for fighting. This did not work out very well. Once the locals found out we were from the Portsmouth area, it would usually kick off. We could not win: if we stayed around Pompey we were marked out as being from Emsworth but when we went further out of our area we were marked out as being from Portsmouth. I see it now all the time in Blackpool: young lads who can not get in to any of the licensed venues in the town centres now, what with Anti Social Behaviour Orders, the pub watch schemes and other local initiatives.

Once, in Bournemouth, we got involved in a scrap outside the roof-top club in the town centre. A large group of lads on a coach party from somewhere kicked off at the end of the night, just as all the clubgoers were leaving. Everyone seemed to be scrapping when this lad threw a bottle that just missed Pete Juggins and myself. We both looked at each other and came to the same decision: this cunt is having it. Both of us chased him down the street, where he vaulted a wall that was about four feet high. Then he screamed. When we looked over the wall the drop on the other side was considerable: possibly fatal, certainly leg-breaking at the least.

It got to be that nearly every weekend that we went

out, one or more of us would be in a scrap. Sometimes we would win and sometimes we would lose but we would always have a laugh. Gang fights were becoming more common, with teams of lads venturing into different areas on the prowl for trouble. Emsworth is a small fishing village, just outside Havant in Hampshire, surrounded by other villages such as Westbourne and Southbourne. These villages had gangs of teenagers just like Emsworth and we would often carry out raids against their youth clubs, as they would against ours.

Havant is a town that incorporates Leigh Park. Leigh Park was at that time said to be the biggest council estate in Europe and was full of gangs of all ages, from skinheads to bikers. A club right in the middle of the estate called the Point Seven was continually changing customers depending on the relative strengths of the various gangs on the estate itself and in the surrounding area, be they bikers or skinheads.

My dad had taken notice of all the fights I was getting into and although he was quite pleased that I could look after myself, he was also very worried about me ending up in trouble with the police, as he had when he was younger. One of his friends ran a boxing club in Water-looville, a small town about five miles from Emsworth. He took me there one Thursday evening. 'Just see if you like it,' he said.

The trainer, a big bloke by the name of Ron, took a look at me and then gave me an old pair of bag gloves. He told me to hit a punch bag that was hanging from the ceiling a few times, so he could watch my balance and technique. After I had done my best to smash the thing to pieces, with no success I might add, Ron told me to 'glove up'. He waved to a lad that was a fair bit smaller and lighter than I was and told him to get ready for a bit of sparring. The lad looked at me and smiled. I remember thinking to myself, don't worry son, I won't hurt you.

Ron had a word with the other kid and then came over to me and said, 'Let's see what you can do.' Anyway, when the bell went I walked out towards the centre of the ring with a smug grin on my face. Then the little twat spent the next couple of minutes knocking me all over the place, without me even hitting him. When they decided that I had had enough, Ron rang the bell to end the round. The little cunt was still smiling and was not even out of breath. I staggered to where Ron and my dad were standing. My dad said, 'Well?' I looked him in the eye and said, 'I want to learn how to do that.'

One day my brother Colin, who is five years older than me, was dabbling in selling used cars when he came home with a black eye and his glasses broken. When my mum questioned him about it, he fobbed her off with some excuse or other.

Later he told me he had sold a car to two lads, who had brought it back when something had gone wrong with it. My brother had explained that the car was sold as seen but the lads would not accept that and had ended up giving Colin a bit of a slap.

About a week later, Peter Juggins and I were in Havant when I saw the car my brother had sold to these lads – a Ford Anglia with wide wheels – parked in a car park. Explaining things to Peter, I then sat on the bonnet of the Anglia and waited. Pete sat on a wall nearby in case the driver was with his pal. My brother had described the car and the lads to me. I knew they were both older than me but by all accounts they were not any bigger and we would have an element of surprise.

I sat on the bonnet of the car for well over one hour until finally this geezer appeared and shouted at me to get the fuck off his car. Walking towards me by himself, carrying some shopping bags, was a guy two or three years older than me, roughly the same height but not as well built as I was.

'Sorry pal, I thought it was my mate's car. Have you just bought it?' I asked, sliding off the bonnet and stepping towards him.

'Yes I fuck...' was as far as he got before I headbutted him back between some parked cars. His nose was spread across his face. I followed up, kicking him straight between the legs and he dropped face-first onto the floor. I bent down and grabbed his hair.

'That was my brother you and your mate beat up. Tell the cunt he will get the same as you when I see him.'

With that I turned away, to the sound of Pete clapping. The cunt only reported it as an attempted mugging but luckily I was never questioned about it and I never saw him or his mate again.

The first time that we were ever involved in a mugging proper was with a queer who tried chatting Pete up when we were in a strange pub (literally). It was a strange pub too; the cheek of it, Pete could have been with me! The bloke tried pulling Pete when he went to the toilet. You should have seen the state of him when he got back to the bar, he was shaking and had turned white. When he told me what had happened I could not stop laughing. We ended up following the poof outside and doing him, in the physical violence way not the sexual way. He ended up giving us his wallet in an attempt to achieve a win-win situation. The trouble was that at that time we did not know what a win-win situation was all about, so we won and he lost.

This led to us going out around Portsmouth, Chichester and even Edinburgh in Scotland, where Pete's mum moved to for a while, using Pete as bait until we managed to hook something. Notice I say 'something', not someone. That was our mentality at the time, we did not see 'queers' as people. It was only when I realised that I could be a lesbian (I love going with other women) that my attitude changed!

We graduated from doing poofs to doing sailors because they would put up a bit more of a fight, making it more dangerous but also more exciting. Also, you could always guarantee they would have money on them. Sometimes it was us that got a good hiding when other sailors came to help their mates; good thing it was the sailors and not from the poofs. We eventually had a few close calls that took the excitement out of this mad hobby and so in the end we decided to look for something a bit more lucrative.

A kid I knew quite well from school got a job working in an office for the Provident in Havant, about four miles from Emsworth. My parents always got loans at Christmas from the Provident and I remembered as a youngster that their agent would call at our house one evening a week to collect instalments from my mum. My pal, who I will call Neil, had been working at this office for a couple of months and told me that every Friday he would be sent to the bank to deposit the money collected from the local agents for that week. It could be anywhere between £800 and £1,500. This was a fortune to us. He asked if I would be interested in doing a snatch job with him. It turned out that he wanted to fuck off and leave home but he was skint and could not afford it. We talked it over and I decided I would have a look at it the following week to see if it was possible.

Opposite the Provident office was a church yard with a lovely pub next to it named The Old House at Home. The following Friday, Pete and I decided to have a few beers in The Old House at Home. We spent most of the afternoon there and it was very nice too. I decided it was not for us. I explained to my friend that it would take at least two people to do it safely: one to hit Neil and take the bag and one to play interference in case some have-a-go hero tried to intervene. The duo would be able to cross the street and cut through the church yard and, as long as they weren't too obvious or followed, would be able to disappear easily enough, but it would mean splitting the money three ways, not two, so it wasn't really worth it. Well, would you believe it, two or three weeks later my mate Neil got turned over: he had just under £1,100 stolen from him. He had to quit his job because of nerves and ended up moving away from the area but he still keeps in touch to this day.

It was not long after that I managed to save up and buy myself a secondhand car. It was an old red Ford Mark 1 GT Cortina with wide wheels and lowered suspension. I loved that car. I think Pete bought himself one around that time as well.

Although I have been charged by the police with numerous serious offences, my only criminal conviction is for actual bodily harm. The four of us – Dave, Mark, Pete and I – had decided to let the Isle of Wight have the benefit of our company for a Saturday evening. We had travelled from Portsmouth Harbour over to Ryde on the Isle of Wight by ferry, all in good humour and decked out in our finest clobber. We went in a few pubs and found out where the best night club was for our taste.

We had been in the club for about an hour and I was having a good time. The first thing I knew about a fight was when this local kid gave Dave a smack. Inevitably it was over a girl. Dave belted the lad who had hit him, knocking him to the floor. The next thing there were lads coming in at us from all directions. We had been through this type of thing quite a few times in the past; so we quickly grouped together and managed to hold our own until the doormen arrived. Guess who got asked to leave?

After the doormen had thrown us out I noticed my

gold chain had been pulled from my neck, so straight away I was back at the front door asking the doormen if I could go back in and look for it. I got the usual answer, 'Sorry son, no chance, but I will go and have a look for it, you wait here.' I thought, yeah right, not a sniff of getting it back.

Five minutes later the doorman came strolling back to the door with a grin on his face. I think to myself, the twat's found it but will say he hasn't. What a surprise I got when he held out his hand with two chains in it. 'One for you and one for me,' he laughed. Good on you mate.

One of the Isle of Wight lads must have seen that we were still outside, because the next minute their firm came piling out and surrounded us. They were more interested in Dave than the rest of us. Their main boy, a tall, well-built lad by the name of Paul Smith, fronted him to have a one-on-one there and then. Dave was a bit weary because he had been fighting again with another one of their lads since we had been evicted but he was still up for it.

They faced off with each other and after some sparring that was not going too well for Dave and some verbal abuse from them slagging us off, I stepped forward and said, 'I'll fight you, you cunt, you're more my size anyway.' I moved in closer, throwing punches with both hands. He grabbed hold of me and we grappled. It was all over after a couple of minutes. He was a big, strong boy but the fear factor had set in with me and that was when I start to perform. It is like taking a drug that enhances my performance. Mind you this only works with violence, if it happens during sex it has the opposite effect. Their boy was on the deck, well and truly fucked. When he had gone down I had picked him up and belted him a few more times. This would come back and bite me when I was in the magistrates court.

We decided to leg it when his pals started to scream

for an ambulance and the police. The four of us ran from the nightclub into a warren of unfamiliar streets. We could hear sirens in the distance getting closer. A police car turned into the street, coming towards us, its headlights and blue flashing light highlighting the four of us. Quick as a flash we were through the gates of a house, across the garden, over a fence and through another garden onto a parallel street. The police would be looking for a group of four lads so we decided to split up into two pairs and make our way to the ferry. Pete and Mark headed off one way and Dave and I the other. Fuck! Fuck! Fuck! We were stuck on an island and there was no ferry until 7am.

We were dodging police cars everywhere we went, jumping over fences and hedges, sometimes through the hedge if it was too high to clear. We ended up crossing some waste ground in the middle of the night. It was so dark that I could only just make out Dave's silhouette. He was saying, 'Follow me Steve.' Then he simply vanished. I could not see him anywhere, so I stopped still and whispered.

'Dave, Dave, where are you?'

I heard a groan from just in front of me but I still could not see him. He had fallen down a bloody great hole.

'I'm not following you down there, you dick,' I said, helping him out while laughing at the same time. We ended up dossing down in someone's greenhouse close to the ferry pier for the rest of the night.

Later that morning, we could see the ferry docking onto the pier head from where we were hiding in a nearby garden. We waited for the disembarking passengers to clear the pier. There was no sign of any coppers about so we decided to chance it. We were cold, tired and miserable but, thinking back now, I cannot believe how naïve we were to think they wouldn't have had someone check the first bloody ferry off the island. Still as you grow older you grow wiser, or is it fatter?

The long and the short of it was they had arrested Mark and Pete earlier that morning. The two of them had made their way straight to the pier and had settled down for a kip. Before long they saw a police car driving along the pier, checking the sheltered seating areas and sheds. They made their way to the very end but with nowhere to hide they had both climbed over the rails and worked their way along a ledge and behind one of the buildings, so they were hidden out of plain sight.

In Peter's own words:

We heard the police car stop and both doors open and close. Two men were talking to each other. We could hear their footsteps getting closer to where we were hiding. All of a sudden a head popped around the corner of the building.

'All right lads, what are you up to then?' asks this copper.

Quick as a flash I reply, 'Fishing officer.'

'Caught much have you?' he asks, shining his torch along the ledge and over the two of us.

I looked at Mark, who was standing in the same position as me, squeezed back against the side of the building with both hands flat against the wall, not a fishing rod or line in sight.

'Right son, full name and date of birth?' asked the first copper.

'Stuart Maguire,' I replied, using a false name.

'How do you spell that,' asks the copper, 'small "c" or big "c"?'

Fuck, I could never spell very well, why didn't I use an easy name like Smith?

'Okay, you've got me, my name is Peter Juggins, spelt J, U, G, G I, N, S.'

As soon as they got us to the police station, they informed us that the disc jockey from the nightclub where the incident had taken place was in fact from the mainland (Hayling Island) and he had already identified our little group, especially a Mr Stephen Sinclair as the person they wished to talk to.

Dave and I were heading towards the gang plank with our tickets in our hands.

'Excuse me gentlemen, could we have a word with you before you board the ferry?'

The voice seemed to come out of nowhere. Turning, both of us saw a couple of uniformed officers of the local constabulary walking towards us. *Bollocks!* We were nicked.

In the end I was the only one charged. I was accused of assault occasioning actual bodily harm. My plea of self-defence was not accepted and I was found guilty in the magistrates court, but with the mitigation that we had been attacked by the locals and that even though I had been defending myself, I had then become the aggressor.

It had also helped me when Mr Smith had turned up to give evidence dressed in a leather jacket, jeans and boots. When he was in the dock, the court heard that he had signed himself out of the hospital on the night in question and was not very helpful at all, although when he was asked if he recognised the person who had injured him, he pointed at me and said, 'Yeah, that fucking gorilla there.'

The magistrates looked at him, at his appearance and his demeanour, then turned to look at me. I was dressed in a nice suit, shirt and tie and looked like butter would not melt in my mouth. I was found guilty but the magistrates agreed that I had been defending myself up until I became the aggressor. The outcome was a £50 fine, a half-decent result considering, but still a criminal conviction.

4

Blackpool Bouncer

WHEN I WAS eighteen, my mum and dad decided they were going to move back up north, but instead of returning to Ashton-under-Lyne they looked at Blackpool. The famous Lancashire town on the north-west coast of England is reported to be the largest seaside resort in Europe. However the town itself is relatively small, with a resident population of about 150,000. One of the things I noticed was that most people I came across had moved there from somewhere else in the country. Most of the lads I would eventually knock around with were from other towns and had moved to Blackpool like me. Some had first come on holiday and stayed, others had just upped and left their homes for a variety of reasons, the most common being female trouble or police trouble.

When we first arrived we lived in a house in neighbouring Cleveleys, a small coastal town a few miles north of Blackpool. Pete and Mark also both came up from Pompey to give it a go but I think they were too southern to settle north of Watford Gap. The first summer saw me get a job as a sports organiser bluecoat at Pontins – but not in Blackpool. Instead I worked at Prestatyn in North Wales. What a job: playing sport all day, shagging every night and getting paid for it. It was only a seasonal job but it was good fun while it lasted.

The first time I was arrested in Blackpool was at a football match. The local team were playing Bristol Rovers. Being bored and not knowing anyone in my new hometown, I decided to go to the football ground at Bloomfield Road and watch the match. I had been there before with Portsmouth FC, in fact I was there when the legend 'Pompey Boot Boys' was sprayed on Bloomfield Road bridge – it remained there for about twenty years and I would always smile when I saw it.

This time I went in the local end, the 'Spion Kop', and was minding my own business when a fight broke out between the home fans and some Bristol lads who had intentionally entered the Blackpool end. I was a strange face to everyone, so I became a target for both sides. I reacted and cleared a space around me by punching and kicking anyone who came near me. All of a sudden a hand grabbed my right shoulder from behind, pulling me around into what I thought would be a punch. As I was being turned I stepped into it and threw a big left hook. *Fuck!* It was only a copper. He landed on his arse with a look of surprise on his face that was probably the same as on mine.

Fuck! Fuck! Fuck! The next thing I knew I was being banged up in the back of a police van for my first visit to Blackpool nick. I was kept in the cells until the Monday morning, when I was brought up in front of the magistrates charged with assault.

Several months later, a headline appeared in the Blackpool *Evening Gazette*: 'Kop Fight Man Acted in Self Defence.' The duty solicitor played up the fact that I had just moved to the area, didn't know anyone, had gone in the wrong end by mistake, been attacked, and so on, and fair play to the arresting officer, he did not make a big deal about the incident. I was acquitted but the downside was that my name was in the Blackpool system now.

I started working the doors to get to know people; it

seemed the easiest way. My first door job was at the Castle Casino on the seafront at North Shore, a members-only casino that, as its name suggests, looks like a castle. I saw an advert in the local *Evening Gazette* and applied for the job, and although I enjoyed it at the time, and stayed there for a few months, ultimately it was not for me. The management wouldn't let me go inside and throw anyone out or bang them, even if they were kicking off. We had to wait until the troublemakers came out and then tell them they were barred. It was a bit frustrating but as only members or the guests of members were allowed in, there was not that much trouble anyway.

The first nightclub in Blackpool that I worked was a different world altogether. I was approached by one of the casino customers, who turned out to be the manager of the Dixieland Club on Central Pier. He asked if I fancied working for him. The 'Dixie' was one of the biggest clubs in the town at that time, along with the famous Mecca on Central Drive, and was rocking every night, mainly with holidaymakers. As you faced the pier, the entrance to the club was in the centre. Glass doors opened to a massive central stairway that was about twenty feet wide. The carpet gave the place a feeling of false grandeur. You walked up the stairs to gain entry to the vast interior, which would invariably be thronged with lads and lasses from all over the country. I was paid about £8 a night but was working with some guys who wouldn't know how to have a fight even if it was put on them, although there was one good lad from Scotland by the name of John.

Early on in my employment, some geezer tried getting in with jeans on, which was against the club policy, so I knocked him back. He started with all the usual shit, 'Do you know who I am, you southern cunt?' I couldn't win; I got it in the neck moving down south and speaking with a Manchester accent, then when I move back up north I talked with a southern accent! Anyway, he then banged me right on the jaw. *Wham!*

Now I have always been able to take a good punch, so I shook my head, looked at him and smiled.

'My turn, dickhead, I said. Then I dropped him with a right cross that also closed his left eye.

'Now fuck off.'

Ten minutes later, I saw a team of geezers crossing the road with dickhead leading the way. The bloke working with me was Mick Tickle, a huge man who stood 6ft 4in and weighed twenty stone. Speaking from the side of my mouth, I said to Tickle, 'Looks like we have a problem.' No answer. I turned round and just caught sight of the big lump disappearing at the top of the stairs.

The lady working behind the cashier's desk asked me, 'What are you going to do Steve?'

'Get a good hiding by the look of it,' I replied.

There was no way I was locking the door or running away like that other cunt. I took a right good beating from this team and was informed in no uncertain terms what would happen to me if I was there the next week-end.

As I tended my wounds afterwards, Billy, the manager, said he wanted me to stay. Though I was not happy with some of the lads I would be working with, I decided I would come back. The next weekend I walked into work wearing a pair of black dealer boots with a cutthroat razor nestling comfortably in each boot. Fuck 'em. If they came after me again, I was not the only one getting hurt.

I continued working there for about a month without any reprisals; but I was still not happy working with the wankers who had left me by myself, so I decided to move on. Some time later, I got to know the bloke that I had had the altercation with quite well and he was okay; he'd had just a drop too much alcohol at the time.

I was now boxing at light-heavyweight for the Fleet-wood Gym ABA club in nearby Fleetwood and for the Bamber Bridge ABA club in Preston. I also started doing a lot of sparring with Brian London and a young heavyweight named Mick Creasy. We would use the boxing ring that Brian had erected in his nightclub, the 007, on Topping Street in central Blackpool. Brian's club was almost as famous as the man himself. The dance floor was about the same size as a small boxing ring and there were four pillars that could be roped off so it could be used for sparring.

Brian London, whose real surname was Harper, was the son of Jack, a former British heavyweight champion. Brian too went on to become British and Commonwealth heavyweight champion and fought both Floyd Patterson and Muhammad Ali, then Cassius Clay, for the championship of the world, although he lost both bouts. He was a fighter, not a boxer, and taught me some very good techniques for brawling in close and dirty. I respect Brian London as a fighter and a man and wish him well always.

I am sure that many books could be written about people like him and another Blackpool man who has my utmost respect, Michael 'Mixie' Walsh. Michael is a local legend and he has appeared in many true crime books, linked with the Kray twins and other gangsters of that era like Eric Mason. But both he and Brian are a lot older than me and my friends and this is our time that I am writing about, although they will pop up in the book now and again.

By day I had started working as a gym instructor and one of the gym customers was the manager of the Mecca Ballroom on Central Drive. He learned that I was a doorman and asked if I wanted to work for him, as he felt his door team was not strong enough. The only interviews bouncers had in those days were: 'How big are you?' and 'Can you fight?' There were no criminal records checks, to training courses and no references asked for. So at the age of twenty, armed with just my two fists and a fighting attitude, I became head doorman at one of the biggest clubs in the country.

The Mecca was huge, with a main ballroom downstairs and any number of bars and function rooms, most famously the upstairs Highland Room, which rivalled Wigan Casino as the main northern soul venue, though the music tended to be funkier than at the more traditional Wigan. We had everything from tea dances to live bands and soul all-nighters, with coach parties pulling up from all over the country.

Although the Mecca was massive, it was in decline because of a chronic lack of investment. The general manager was a man named Graham Peel and the under-managers were David Howe and Ted Scantlebury. Ted was a big half-caste fellow who helped with security and had perfected a flick with the outside of his hand into the testicles of a miscreant, which would bring down the offender's chin just in time to meet Ted's crunching elbow strike. It rarely failed. The problem was that we had only about half a dozen doormen to handle sometimes thousands of customers. There was no way we could separate two coach parties slugging it out, but we did our best. The accepted ratio these days is one doorman per hundred customers but back then there were no rules.

One night we had over three thousand customers in the building with a total of six door staff. Talk about a recipe for trouble; all six of us ended up at the Blackpool Victoria Hospital accident and emergency room, along with approximately thirty of our customers. It was kicking off everywhere, complete chaos, and we were losing one doorman at a time. We got them all out in the end but all ended up with a trip to casualty. Fortunately in those days fights rarely resumed at the hosiptal, as people seemed to have more respect for the doctors and nurses than they do now.

Sex and violence became the main things in my life. I actually started two rumours around that time: one that I was a good shag, and the other that I was a good fighter. Only one managed to last the distance, guess which one. *Bastard!*

I met a Blackpool girl by the name of Jacqueline Curry whom I thought I was in love with at the time and after a short engagement we were married. On June 1, 1979, Jackie gave me a beautiful baby daughter who we named Kelly. At that time Kelly was the be-all and end-all for me; she was a wonderful baby with a beautiful nature, and she has matured into a beautiful woman.

Trying to bring some security into our life, I decided to join the Army. With my passion for fitness, I wanted to be a physical training instructor. I had thought you could get straight into the Army Physical Training Corps if you represented your county in a sport but I was informed at the Army careers office that you had to join a regular regiment first and if you were outstanding in a sport or during physical training you might get offered the opportunity to become an assistant instructor in the gym with that regiment. After twelve months, if you were good enough, you would then be offered the opportunity of a transfer to the Army Physical Training Corps.

In 1979, I joined the Royal Engineers and was sent to Gibraltar Barracks in Camberley near Aldershot. One of the first things you are asked when you join your regiment is, 'Are you any good at a sport?' As soon as I mentioned boxing I was told to report to a Warrant Officer Kelly, who ran the boxing team, and the regiment sergeant major, who was the chief coach. The boxing team would travel into Aldershot and spar with lads who were in the Parachute Regiment. Those sparring sessions were as hard as any bouts I ever took part in. The Paras always believed they had something to prove and if you beat one of them there would be a queue of them outside the ring waiting for their turn to get at you.

Things went well for me. I became the regiment's light-heavyweight champion, winning all my fights, and also got elected as the captain of the boxing team. Everything was going great and I was even offered the position of assistant gym instructor at the Gibraltar Barracks. This would have gained me an instant promotion to lance-corporal and after twelve months a transfer to the Army Physical Training Corps. But something always happens to put a spanner in the works.

Family problems soon became a major issue in my personal life; certain things happening back in Blackpool came to light. I was granted compassionate leave to try to sort it out but things got worse, not better. It resulted in me obtaining an early discharge from the Army and eventually filing for a divorce from Jackie.

When I got back to Blackpool I was not sure what I wanted to do. But I needed work and so I ended up back on the doors in Blackpool, working at the busy Foxhall pub on the promenade with a very good friend of mine, Robin Thompson. Robin played professional football before an injury caused him to change career. During the day he ran a pawnbrokers on Central Drive, a long thoroughfare the runs parallel to the prom, but Robin is a very physical guy – he is about five feet ten inches tall, has a very stocky build, a knockout punch in both hands and the biggest calves I have seen on a man – and he was drawn to working as a doorman for a bit of excitement. He had previously asked me for a job at the Mecca.

In those days the pubs were open from eleven o'clock in the morning through to three o'clock in the afternoon, then they would reopen at six until eleven at night. These hours applied Monday to Saturday. On Sunday they changed to noon through to two o'clock and then seven to ten-thirty. You can imagine the fun that door staff would have: at twenty past two on a Sunday afternoon you had to move large teams of Geordies or Scousers out of the pub when it was pissing down outside and there was nowhere for them to go.

Robin had vouched for me to get me the job at the

Foxhall but when I turned up the landlord, Bill Robinson, looked at me with some scepticism. I was twelve and a half stone, baby faced and wore a black velvet jacket and a black velvet bow tie that was the height of fashion at the time. When I look at some of the photographs from that era now, I cringe myself. Big Bill, who was an ex-professional boxer, could not weigh me up but it was not long before I had the chance to prove myself.

One afternoon it came on top with a big Scottish geezer. I had not been involved in any fights there yet, and I knew it. The lads at the door tried to stop this big geezer coming in, but he was having none of it and pushed past Gary Wade and Robin.

I was stood just inside the pub and stepped forward when I heard the commotion. I stepped straight into the path of this geezer and said, 'Hold it pal,' stopping him in his tracks. He looked at me and laughed, then he placed his hand on my chest to push me out of the way. Now when I say he was a big geezer, I mean he was big. My heart was racing and he could feel it because he laughed again and said in a loud voice, 'You're shitting yourself.' Then he tried to push me out of his way.

Now I don't know about you but when I get scared or nervous, that is when I step up a bit and start performing. So as he stepped forward, I headbutted him with everything I had, right in the middle of his face. He dropped like a brick, straight down. Robin and Gary grabbed an arm each, dragged him outside and left him. The other door lads and Big Bill came over to see what was happening. I was just managing to calm down when all of a sudden he was back, large as life but a lot uglier with his nose spread all over his face. He was not laughing any more and boy, was he angry.

'I want fucking Blondie,' he was shouting pointing at me. 'Get that cunt out here.'

Now I was stood inside the door, with four other doormen and Big Bill between me and him. I was thinking, fuck you pal, you're not getting me out there, when out of nowhere Big Bill the landlord says, 'Get out there and do him Steve.'

'Do what?'

Robin looked me in the eye and said, 'You had better do it Steve or he will sack you.'

This big guy was out there now jumping up and down. When he spotted me taking off my jacket and bow tie he started shouting what he was going to do to me, how he was going to rip off my head and shit down my neck.

I walked out onto the pavement, all the time looking at this big bastard, thinking, fuck, fuck, fuck. I could see his mates grinning behind him. He looked me in the eye and must have thought he had already won; he started posing, sticking his fucking huge chest out and looking around at his pals.

I stepped forward and kicked him as hard as I could in his bollocks. Whoosh, he deflated like a punctured balloon, dropping to his knees where I delivered a few right hands to finish the job. Thank fuck for that. I turned around to see Robin saying to Big Bill, 'I told you he could do a bit.'

That season on the door of the Foxhall was a learning experience. You get teams of lads and ladies from all over the country coming to Blackpool either on day trips or for stag and hen do's. Most of them are there to have a good time but you always get the ones that want to spoil it for the others.

One Saturday afternoon, Gary Wade was on the door knocking back some lads. I was not really taking a lot of notice at the time, we were too busy inside the venue, but I did a fast double-take: one of the blokes Gary was knocking back was only Dave 'Boy' Green, the British and European welterweight champion, who had fought both Carlos Palomino and Sugar Ray Leonard for the world title, although both times unsuccessfully. He was still one of my favourite British fighters. I soon showed some interest then, I promise you. Making sure Dave and his friends got in okay, I managed to spend some time in his company. What a lovely fellow.

A lot of people are beaten by someone's reputation before the fight begins. When you are willing to work a door on Blackpool promenade, however, you are going to meet people from all walks of life that you have never heard of and who have never heard of you. What you see is what you get. In general, most people seem to think that someone who looks hard is hard. Sometimes this is true and they can do a bit but a lot of the time it's not. They can look that way because they have taken a lot of second prizes.

We became used to blokes looking at us and talking amongst themselves, then coming over to one of us and asking, 'What would you do if he started causing trouble?' and pointing over to a bruiser who was with them. Most of the time, depending on what type of mood we were in, we would make a joke about it so as not to cause any trouble. Other times we would look over at the individual in question, smile and say, 'Knock him out.' As you can imagine this did not go down well and we would usually end up battling.

Those were the days when doormen were known as bouncers. I knew some bouncers that would see lads in nice clothes or shoes and would stand next to them to see if they would fit. If they did, later that evening some excuse for throwing them out would be fabricated and voila, the bouncer had some new clobber. Luckily the new legislation that has been brought in over the past few years has managed to clear a lot of these guys out of the security industry. We would often end up facing coachloads of lads on day trips that were there for a shag or a fight. When they were too pissed to get a shag, they could always come to see us for a fight. In those days, bouncers always had bats or sawn-off snooker cues close at hand.

One day the front door of the Foxhall came under siege from a large number of angry miners from Yorkshire or Newcastle. I can't remember what started the incident but it soon got out of hand. The doors at the front and side were shut, with this group outside trying to smash their way in. They could not get in but the pub was still full of customers who wanted to get out. We were stuck.

Either Big Bill or Robert Houston, whoever was in charge that day, decided enough was enough, we were to tool up and open the doors. One tactic we had used before when we had a mob kicking off at the front entrance was to close the doors, then arm ourselves with pool cues and bats and charge out of another door at the side of the pub, coming around and catching the troublemakers unawares. All the bar staff were males and most of them were from Scotland so they were all up for it. The tills were secured and the doors were opened, all we needed was police uniforms and it would have looked like a scene from the miners' strike that was all over the news at that time. Some of us eventually found ourselves fighting outside the Manchester pub, which is a good two hundred yards from the Foxhall. It was like a rolling scrum all the way down the promenade, a heaving mass of bodies with arms, legs and the occasional weapon all thrashing away. We legged it back when the police eventually turned up – I think Robin actually jumped in a passing taxi back to the Foxhall – and there were no comebacks, as in those days the police took a much more lenient line on doormen fighting on the pavement.

A funny story from that era was on a weekend when a large number of deaf and dumb visitors congregated at the Foxhall. The pub was full with music playing but obviously no-one speaking, though there was a lot of sign language going on. I had been getting a lot of eye contact from this cute-looking deaf and dumb girl. One thing led to another and we were in the cleaning cupboard, where a quick kiss and cuddle turned to full-on sex. Just as I was enjoying myself she started screaming, no words, just 'Haaawaaa' over and over. I shit myself; thinking, what the fuck, people will think I am raping her. That was it; I pulled out, zipped up and jumped out of the cupboard. No-one was taking any notice as obviously they hadn't heard a thing! Re-entry was quickly resumed.

5

Sugar Ray

ONE SATURDAY I was working the door at the Foxhall when a friend of mine and Robin's named Wayne Hyrons came into the pub with his sister and a bloke I did not know. Wayne and his sister were both working on the *Queen Elizabeth 2* as catering staff and the bloke with them, John Hillier, also worked on the luxury liner. Wayne was aware that I had worked on the *QE2* previously and had come into the pub to see me. It turned out that John was also the union shop steward for the *QE2* and had good contacts with Cunard, the company that owned the ship. After talking for a while, John gave me the name and telephone number of his contact at Cunard and told me to ring him the following week. He offered me a job on the *QE2* as a silver service waiter. Thinking long and hard about what I had going for me at that time – shagging and fighting being about it – I decided to accept the offer and before long I was on my way down to Southampton to rejoin the *QE2*.

Ships are always known as 'she'; I don't know why this is, unless it is because they can go down on you. The *Queen Elizabeth 2* was at that time one of the biggest, and certainly the most prestigious, cruise liners in the world, with four restaurants, numerous bars, a night club and casino, about a dozen shops, outdoor and indoor swimming pools, a fully equipped gym and even a cinema.

Quite a few lads and girls from Blackpool were working on the ship when I rejoined, including a close friend of mine called Steve Marsh, who was a petty officer in the engineering department. The last time I had been on board I was only a junior rating and I had not realised how much antagonism there was between the deck hands, catering and engineering crew.

Gordon Phillips was still the *Queen's* queen, if you know what I mean, so I planned on keeping my head down below his radar. Amongst one thousand crew members on a ship that big you would think 'no problem', but no, not me. The first time the ship docked back in New York, me, Wayne and another lad from Blackpool named Ian Lucock were walking back to the ship down Forty-Second Street when one of the junior waiters approached us in tears. He had saved up his money to buy himself a ghettoblaster and no sooner had he left the store than he had been mugged. At that time Forty-Second Street was notorious for black gangs robbing or fleecing tourists and the like.

'Walk with us, you will be okay,' we said, feeling really sorry for him.

Ten yards further on down the street, we are approached by two black men, both quite tall but not heavy in build.

'Hey man, you want to buy?' said the one coming up on my right side. As soon as I turned to face him, the one on my left grabbed my gold chain from my neck and took off up the street. At that time I was as fit as a butcher's dog and anyway I always could sprint. I caught him within about ten yards and banged him into a shop front. I hit him with a couple of shots as he bounced back at me and he went down.

'Steve, I've got your chain, he dropped it,' came the shout from Wayne.

I looked around at my pals and then back at the guy at my feet. 'You prick,' I said, then I phlegmed up and spat at him.

Walking back towards the others, the second mugger confronted me, pulling off his shirt. I presume this was to show me how ripped his muscles were. He went into a karate or kickboxing pose, no doubt influenced by the Bruce Lee movies that were popular at the time. A high side-kick nearly took my head off but just missed me as I swayed to the side. My right uppercut didn't miss and nearly took his balls off; it lifted him clear off the ground and left him squirming in a heap on the sidewalk (that's American for pavement). I was about to stick my boot into the cunt's head when one of my mates shouted a warning. Looking around I saw loads of black youths who seemed to be coming out of the woodwork, I swear they were just materialising out of nowhere.

'What shall we do?' one of the others shouted.

Looking back, I shouted, 'Fucking run,' and I took off like there was a load of cannibals after me. We ran down Forty-Second Street towards the docks. Like four snowflakes being chased by a giant oil slick, we were slowly but surely being overhauled.

'In here lads,' shouted a big lump of a white man standing outside a doorway, just as we were about to be chased down and caught. As we dashed into the building we were nearly pushed back out by big hefty geezers coming to the doorway. It turned out to be an Irish bar where the locals were all stevedores (dockyard workers) who loved to have a fight with the local blacks now and again.

'They won't come in here,' said one of the blokes blocking the doorway.

After we had explained what had caused us to be in full flight down Forty-Second Street, we were treated to a couple of glasses of Guinness and a few funny stories.

Once back onboard the *QE2*, I had to report to sick bay. I had gashed the knuckles on my right hand when I had hit the first bastard. Obviously I had caught him in the mouth and with luck I thought I might have knocked some of his teeth down his throat.

Anyone who has worked on board a ship will know how fast a story like that can spread among the crew. I had tried to keep my history of being a bouncer and having done some boxing quiet, simply because of the bad feeling that existed between the deckhands, engineers and the catering crew.

As when I was younger, there is always a pecking order, especially on a confined ship with one thousand crew on board. Within no time I was being singled out by deckhands or engineers who fancied themselves in a scrap. They had the idea that all the catering staff were poofs; okay, a lot of them were, but there was also a lot of ex-Forces personnel who joined the ship as catering because that was the easiest way to do so. There were quite a few blokes on board who kept themselves to themselves who were ex-Special Forces or experts in martial arts. It does not matter where you go, for every hard man you actually come across there are at least three that are just as good, if not better, that you will never hear of.

Once everything settled down I ended up doing quite well for myself. I went from working as a waiter in the restaurants to being a room and deck steward. I then got promoted to second storekeeper, which is petty officer rank. After about twelve months I was promoted to petty officer in charge of the public rooms, a high-profile position looking after all the stewards that worked in the bars and public rooms.

Soon after, the ship made its inaugural visit to Philadelphia on the east coast of America. The ship docked in the so-called City of Brotherly Love for one day only and then was due to take a three-day cruise with a full complement of passengers. Sailing time was about six o'clock in the evening.

I went ashore in Philly with two lads from the Bristol area who worked in my department, Andy and Mick. We were soon having a great time in one of the city's many shady bars with some of the local ladies. From the bar we were in we had a wonderful view of the Delaware River. All of a sudden, there was the *QE2* sailing out to sea: we had missed the ship. Leaving the bar pronto, we started back to the dock, all thinking, what the fuck shall we say? With there being three of us together, we had to come up with a story that covered all of us.

The best idea was that we had been mugged, so straight away we phoned 911 and reported it; the area we were in was a bit suspect anyway. As we waited for the police to arrive, we decided we needed some bruises for it to look real. I told the two lads to attack me and I would defend myself, that way we would all have some marks or bruises. As they both stepped forward, I hit the one on my left with a right cross and the other with a left hook. The poor cunts both went down, one with his nose spread across his face and the other with a broken jaw. Shit! I haven't got a mark on me. I was stood there telling them to get up and to hit me when I heard a siren getting closer and closer. Neither of the two lads was up for it so in the end I had to take off one of my shoes and belt myself in the face a few times. By the time the police arrived I was sufficiently bruised to satisfy them that we were all victims of a mugging.

Both of the other lads were taken to hospital where they made statements saying that I had protected them after they had been knocked down by a gang of coloured lads. The police drove me around the area looking for the gang, we even went into some very dodgy bars where heavily armed police told me not to worry and if I saw anybody that I recognised just point at them and they would cuff them and take them in for questioning. I was very tempted a couple of times but in the end I just said that I could not recognise anyone. I think they thought that I was scared. The barmen in some of the places remembered us from being in their bars earlier that afternoon and this seemed to confirm our story.

The police contacted Cunard, who informed the *QE2*. Cunard put me up in a lovely hotel where I was later joined by Andy. He wouldn't leave the hotel room because he was a vain bastard and his nose was a mess. Mick had to have surgery on his jaw and remained in the hospital until the ship docked back in Philadelphia three days later. Both of them were taken off the duty roster and put on sick leave. I returned to my duties as the public room supervisor. On the following trip, I was only introduced to all of the passengers at the captain's cocktail party and given an award from Cunard for bravery. Fuck me!

Boredom is a big problem on board ships. That is why so many of the crew become pissheads and turn into alcoholics. Fitness was a big part of my life at that time, mainly to combat the boredom. When we docked in a foreign port, if I was off duty I would go for a run. In New York I would run from the ship to Central Park, through the park and back. It was great and I was soon joined by one or two of my mates which made it even more enjoyable.

I approached the staff captain and asked for some money from the crew sports and social fund to buy some boxing equipment. The staff captain knew that there was a lot of tension between the different departments and made a deal with me: if he gave me the money to buy the equipment, it would be made available to all members of the crew and I would have to be willing to train with them if I was available. Quickly I agreed and the staff captain gave me $1,000 to buy some boxing and fitness equipment.

This proved to be a great success, bringing the different departments together and easing a lot of tension on board the ship. I would spend two or three hours a day in a five-deck annex, working out on the punch bags, sparring with crew members who had boxed before and teaching people who had never boxed. Before long, crew members proficient in other forms of martial arts were training with us and swapping techniques.

One day as I was going about my duties I heard a voice boom from the public address system: 'Will Stephen Sinclair please report to the staff captain.'

Fuck me, I thought, *what have I done now?*

When I got to the staff captain's office, the Cruise Director, who was in charge of passenger entertainment, was there with him. It turned out that the famous Sugar Ray Leonard, at that time the light-middleweight champion of the world, was coming on board the *QE2* in the very near future to sail from New York to Southampton. There would be a documentary film crew with him and they had asked if there was anyone on board who could train with him and possibly take part in an exhibition bout. The staff captain had remembered my request for boxing equipment and immediately thought of me.

So would I be interested?

Fucking yes! Too right I would.

To me Sugar Ray Leonard was the most exciting boxer of that era. The way he had beaten Thomas Hearns and then destroyed Dave 'Boy' Green, the British boxer, fucking right I was interested.

They gave me a date that was just two weeks away. The staff captain offered me the use of all passenger amenities, including the menu, but I was fucked again. He was offering me unlimited amounts of some of the best scran you could ever eat at a time when I had to lose weight! For the next two weeks I was a regular sight to the passengers running up and down the main stairs, from the boat deck down to five deck, the lowest passenger deck, and back up again. I would spar with whoever was available at any time, night or day; it was like something out of the film 'Rocky'.

The day finally came when we docked in New York to pick up Sugar Ray and his party. I was as excited as a ten-year-old on Christmas morning waiting to unwrap my presents. At our first meeting I was a little awestruck.

This got even worse after training with him. His speed was unbelievable and his punches would crack like a whip against the punchbag or pads. I felt like a horse that pulled a milk cart standing next to a thoroughbred racehorse.

Ray, though still light-middleweight champ, had undergone surgery on a detached retina. It had been successful and he was looking at a possible fight against Marvelous Marvin Hagler, the undisputed middleweight champion. He would watch me on the pads or the bag and one time came over and asked me how I was on body shots. I hooked a few into the bag and looked at him. He smiled at me and said, 'I meant taking them.' Then he laughed and went back to skipping. He could make a skipping rope sing; I had never seen anyone use a rope like that before. He would change hands whilst jumping then take both handles in one hand and whip the rope in a figure-eight pattern faster than the eye could see, then without stopping would switch back to both hands and resume skipping.

Our exhibition bout was to take place in the main passenger show room on the upper deck, with up to two thousand passengers and quite a few crew members watching. There was also the documentary team filming us. So no pressure then!

The master of ceremonies introduced me to the crowd as 'the heavyweight champion of the Queen Elizabeth the Second, the Rocky of the lower decks'. He then went on to say that I could become a legend in the pubs, factories and dockyards of Blackpool – obviously he did not know any-thing about Blackpool. Talk about feeling embarrassed.

Then it came over the speakers: 'In the other corner we have the welterweight and light-middleweight champion of the world, Sugar Ray Leonard.' Even I was cheering for him!

We came together in the centre of the ring and touched gloves. I towered over him but for some inexplicable reason he did not appear worried. I had been told not to hit his head with any big right hands because of his previous eye injury. I wasn't sure I would get near enough to hit him with anything, let alone a big right.

In the first round I just played with him, teasing him, moving in and out before he could catch me. Not! It was the other way around – he was doing that to me. But in the second round I finally got the better of my nerves and was moving a lot more sharply. I had loosened up. He moved towards me. I stepped back and imitated Leonard's bolo swing with my right, then caught him with a fast hard left jab to his eye. Oh fuck! The pain, shit it hurt – no, not him, me. He got focused and hit me with a left hook to the body, right on the floating rib, not once but twice. I was down, the referee Ollie Dunlap was counting over me, when the bell went for the end of the round.

Ollie pulled me upright and put my arms outstretched straight onto his shoulders.

'Breathe,' he said.

'I'm trying,' I gasped.

Just as I started to get some air into my lungs, a bell sounded and Ollie stepped back and said, 'Go on.'

I looked at him and asked, 'Go on where?'

'Round three,' he smiled, pushing me forward.

You've got to laugh, haven't you?

We ended up doing five rounds, with me now keeping my elbows well tucked in to protect my ribs. I was not going to go through that amount of pain again.

The thing that makes me laugh is when I tell people about it, they ask, 'Who won?' I smile and say, 'Who is one of the most famous boxers of all time, worth tens of millions of pounds? And who is working on the doors in Blackpool?'

Who do you think fucking won?

Sugar Ray Leonard was interviewed by *The Ring* magazine, the bible of boxing, after his later victory over the great Marvin Hagler fight and he mentioned the trip on the *QE2* and me hitting him during our exhibition bout. Leonard stated that for a big man I had fast hands and a real hard punch. After that punch had landed and Ray realised that he could still see out of his eye, he knew then that he would be able to go on and fight Hagler some time in the future. So you could say I literally had a hand in his success!

I have been over to America a few times since then to see Ray fight and more recently met up with him in England, at Old Trafford in Manchester. Top man Ray, thanks for the memories.

One of the funniest things from my time on the *QE2* happened not long after the Sugar Ray Leonard episode. The ship docked in Kowloon, Hong Kong. I was off duty that night and went ashore with one of my mates from Blackpool, Steve Marsh. We took the Star Ferry from Kowloon to Hong Kong and proceeded to try to drink the place dry. The next thing I know, we are in a tattoo parlour getting tattoos. I ended up with two, one on each shoulder. They even sold beer in the parlour so we carried on drinking there.

By the time we staggered to the Star Ferry termi-nal we had missed the last boat. We were both on duty first thing the next morning, so in a drunken haze we decided we would try sailing one of the low-sided Chinese boats called sampans that were moored in the harbour. We chose one at random and pulled it in by its line. As I jumped on board, a hatch opened and a little head appeared. It started screaming at me in Chinese and nearly made me fall overboard. Steve was laughing so much he let go of the rope and the boat started to drift back out. So now I'm shouting at him, the little Chinese head is shouting at me and Steve's falling over laughing.

Once I had managed to get safely off the boat we ended up back at the pier and found a small hut that was unlocked. I woke up freezing cold and with a splitting headache from too much beer. I could not understand where I was or why my shoulders were both hurting, I looked around and saw Steve huddled up in one of the corners covered up by newspapers. Then it all came back to me in a flash. *Oh God.*

I woke Steve and we left the hut and caught the first ferry back to Kowloon. When I explained the story to my boss, he asked, 'Why didn't you get a taxi?'

I must have looked disgusted when I replied, 'Because Hong Kong is an island, duh!'

'They opened the Eastern Harbour tunnel from Kowloon to Hong Kong last year, you dickhead,' he laughed. Well it had been a few years since my last visit.

Another funny incident happened to one of the waiters in the first class restaurant. We were on a world cruise heading from Los Angeles to Hawaii, and as we were docked at Honolulu, the waiter asked his table of Japanese passengers what they had planned for the day. They answered that they were going to visit Pearl Harbour. The waiter, quick as a flash, asked, 'Do they know you are coming this time?' He was sacked the same day and flown home. Although it was obviously not great for him, it did make the rest of the crew chuckle for quite some time.

I enjoyed my time on the ship and made some good pals, lads like Paul Rumble from Bournemouth and Gary Newborn from near Grimsby. We played rugby for the ship team all over the world in such places as Fiji, New Zealand and Japan. In Japan we played in the shadow of Mount Fuji, the volcano. It was awesome. We also toured some of the best whorehouses in the world but I won't go into that. I still meet up regularly with both Paul and Gary and have attended both lads' weddings.

We worked for three months on duty and one month

off and it was during one of my leave periods from the ship that I met Tanee. I had gone to a nightclub located at a country club just outside Blackpool called the Illawalla. My friend Robin Thompson from the Foxhall pub was working there as the head doorman, along with Gary Wade and Dave Thorpe, both also friends. Robin introduced me to the cashier, Tanee, and when our eyes met that was me finished. I thought she was lovely then and I still do today. She is one of the best things that has ever happened to me. My time on the *QE2* was coming to an end.

I returned to the ship at the end of my leave having decided to hand in my notice. We flew into New York to rejoin the *QE2* for the start of a world cruise but what I had not taken into consideration was that I was under company contract to Cunard and was expected to do a full three months' notice. I was gutted. I tried approaching Gordon Phillips, who was the hotel manager at that time, but being the bad queen that he was he refused to let me finish my tour early. I did not want to upset any passengers, as it was not their fault I wanted to get off the ship and they did not want their holiday ruined by me, plus you should never burn your bridges, you just don't know when you may need them again. But there had to be some way off the bloody ship. So I refused to turn up for work, just point blank refusing even when they told me I had to stay with the ship all the way back to Southampton whether I worked or not.

Gordon Phillips had a new boyfriend, a waiter in one of the first class restaurants, and apparently he was like a lovesick puppy. All of a sudden I knew how I was going to get home. One evening I walked into the gay bar, called The Castaways (yes, they had their own bar). The barman was a guy named Johnny Law, a proper old seadog. He looked at me in surprise and asked what I was doing in The Castaways. I just smiled and asked if Gordon Phillips's boyfriend was in the bar. He nodded over to a group of men and pointed him out to me.

I approached the group and asked the lad to stand up. He did. I knocked him out with one punch and said to his friends, 'Tell him Steve Sinclair did it.' Then I turned around, said, 'Goodnight, John,' and left.

Early the next morning I was woken by two masters at arms, the ship's police, knocking on my cabin door. They said the hotel manager wanted to see me.

Gordon Phillips wanted to know what his boyfriend had done to upset me. I told him, 'Nothing, nothing at all.'

'So why did you hit him?' he asked.

'Because I want to get off this ship and you won't let me, so every time I see him from now on I am going to hit him,' I said, looking him straight in the eyes.

It worked. I was flown home from Tokyo but on the condition that I did not try to claim my full wages for the rest of the three months due on the contract.

6

Secrets

I WAS BACK in Blackpool and working on the doors again. Tanee and I got engaged and I moved into her flat on Raikes Parade, just outside the town centre. Everything seemed to be going well.

When I had first met Tanee, she had been in a fairly long-term relationship with a local CID officer (no accounting for taste, eh?). In meeting me she had obviously seen the light, or been converted to the dark side. However, everywhere we went there were bloody coppers coming up to Tanee and saying hello, trying to give her a cuddle or a kiss on the cheek. I ended up losing my temper a couple of times – only with the leery ones – and gave out a couple of right-handers. I was very lucky not to get nicked. One time at Bunters nightclub in Blackpool I was approached by this bloke in a suit, who started talking to me while at the same time poking me in the chest with his finger. I couldn't hear a word that he was saying but I could feel the poking. Poke, poke, poke.

Bang! I hit him with a right hand, knocking him on his arse. Then someone grabs me in a bear hug from behind and drags me to the reception area nearby. The cunt that I have just dropped gets up and follows us. The gorilla who has hold of me is one of the doormen, who had seen me bang the guy. The bloke I had punched reaches into his pocket and pulls a warrant card out and starts to say, 'I am arresting you for assault.'

Just as he does so, Mick Creasy, one of my old boxing mates, comes through the door. He was now the head doorman at Bunters. 'Fucking let him go,' he orders the doorman holding me. Mick did not really know what was happening and, as soon as the doorman let go, I threw a right hand that knocked the copper clean out. With a quick wink and a smile at Mick, I was off.

Mick and the management of the club spent quite a few hours at the police station being questioned as to my identity, but all Mick told them was that I had just asked him for a job and he thought I was a Cockney because I spoke funny. Thanks pal! As for me and Tanee, it took some time and a fair bit of effort on both our parts, but we moved on and we are still together now twenty-three years later.

I was working back at the Foxhall at weekends but also got a job working at TVR, the sports car manufacturer, during the day. I had worked there before and it paid a decent wage but it was not the type of job I would like to be permanent. They were a good bunch of lads but I felt the glass fibre in the body shop where I worked would end up doing my lungs in if I stayed there too long.

It was while I was working at the Foxhall I met Ian Sharples. Ian is as tall as me, if not a bit taller, but has a slimmer build. He had not long been released from prison. Ian had been a doorman at a club called Diamond Lil's at the Pleasure Beach, the huge amusement park on Blackpool promenade which was then reputed to be the busiest single tourist attraction in Europe. A team of lads from Manchester had been either knocked back or thrown out of the club and had returned tooled up with axes and Stanley knives. They attacked the door, badly injuring one of the bouncers.

The doorman who was savagely slashed and hacked was a lad named Pat Wallace. Pat has two brothers, Billy and Jimmy. The Wallaces are originally from Scotland and are all well-known names in the Blackpool area. Pat Wallace was taken to hospital in a very serious condition, while the police closed the club down and took statements from everyone there.

Meanwhile Jimmy Wallace and Ian Sharples went looking for the gang responsible. The trouble was that they went looking with a shotgun. I believe Ian was driving the car, with Jimmy in the back. They drove up and down Blackpool promenade until they recognised the men involved in the attack on Pat. As they did a u-turn, Jimmy wound down the rear window and let the twin barrels of the twelve-bore shotgun poke out. As they drew level with the gang, Jimmy let them have both barrels one after the other, bang, bang. Luckily for Jimmy and Ian – and for the Manchester gang – Jimmy was not used to firing a shotgun and so the recoil of the gun sent the pellets high. Although some of the gang were injured none were killed. A rather large hotel window was 'killed', though. Ian and Jimmy were both found guilty of attempted murder and both served time at Her Majesty's pleasure, Ian getting about four years and Jimmy slightly longer. Pat Wallace went on to make a full recovery but still bears the reminder of that night with some major scars.

At the time that Ian and I met, he played ice hockey for the Blackpool Seagulls and liked to keep fit, so it wasn't long before we started going to the gym together. I soon got him interested in boxing. He had a natural flair for it, could move well and hit hard with both his left and right hand.

Mick Creasy, the head doorman who had helped me out with the copper at Bunters, had opened his own boxing gym in a small town called Thornton, just outside Blackpool. He contacted me and asked if I fancied helping him to train some local amateur boxers. Some of these lads went on to fight for the England or county amateur boxing teams, while others turned professional, lads like Dougie Isles, Richard Leece and Simon McDougal. I jumped at it, as it would also help to keep me fit and sharp. I really enjoyed that period of my life, especially travelling to the different shows with lads like Matt Bridge and Danny McBride. It also gave me the opportunity to train as much as I liked.

Ian would come to the gym with me and his own boxing ability improved greatly. I have always stressed to lads that have worked on the doors with me that fitness is vital. Not only does it help you defend yourself, but also it helps you to think better in stressful situations. And if it still comes on top you have the stamina to leg it, especially if it's from the Old Bill.

As an individual starting to get a reputation, you seem to be fighting all of the time, be it on the door or when you are having a night out. People start talking about you and the fights you have been in and, believe me, in a town the size of Blackpool you only have to fart and the police know about it. The thing with me is I have always tried my best to be fair. I have never taken a liberty. I have the reputation of being a hard man but I am liked and respected by the people that know me, not feared like some others seem to enjoy.

When you work in door security and you get that kind of reputation, it is not long before businessmen start approaching you and asking if you can collect an outstanding debt or two for them. Other people will approach you about someone who has taken a liberty with a family member and ask if you can you do something about it. Obviously they will make it worth your while. If you start taking these jobs on, they can build your reputation even higher, especially if you are successful at them. The trouble is that with this type of work you are putting yourself on the front line. It can become personal and if that happens you can land yourself in a whole heap of trouble. Demanding money with menaces, aggravated burglary, theft: these are the types of charges you can end up facing in court.

Strangers started to say hello to me as I walked past them and I wouldn't have a clue who they were. People also started to use my name to try to get into clubs or to intimidate others when I knew nothing about it. It became a standing joke in Blackpool about how many 'nieces' and 'nephews' I had. In fact one night my eldest daughter Kelly nearly had a fight with a girl who said she was my niece. I have had stories told to me by people who did not know who I was, about things that I was supposed to have done or been involved in, and to tell you the truth I didn't know what they were on about.

This happens all across the country to people with reputations. Stories get exaggerated or fabricated and do the rounds. The next thing you know you are getting pulled in to the police station and questioned about all sorts of things, from armed blags to contract hits.

One evening I called in to The Business nightclub in Blackpool and was talking to the owner, Mike Nordwin, when one of the doormen brought a man over to us.

'Steve, this bloke's trying to use your name to get in.'

He was a stocky guy about thirty and I looked at him and asked, 'Do I know you?'

He looked me right in the eye and said, 'I'm a friend of Steve Sinclair's.'

'I'm Steve Sinclair.'

'No you're not,' he said, straight to my face.

I looked at Mike Nordwin and the doorman that had brought him over. They were both grinning like Cheshire cats.

In the end I had the guy crying and telling me how sorry he was. It goes to prove my point that people will use your name for all sorts of crap.

A similar incident occurred not too long ago at the Blue nightclub in Blackpool. I was looking after the club when some of our younger customers came over to me nearly in tears. When I asked them what the matter was, they replied that they had been searched in the toilets by a strange bloke who was not part of the door team.

I asked them to point out the individual as we walked around the club. They soon spotted him and, sure enough, there he was actually searching someone else. I pulled him to one side.

'What do you think you're doing?'

Again, the man looked me straight in the eye and said, 'Steve said it is okay for me to search people.'

'Steve who?' I asked.

'Steve Sinclair,' he replied

'I'm Steve Sinclair.'

He growled, 'Fuck off.'

I gave him 'fuck off'. I knocked the clown straight through the fire escape and down the stairs.

Pretty soon you start getting the blame for all sorts of things. The police would pull me in for questioning and inevitably my girlfriend and even my parents would be asking me if I had been involved in this incident or that incident. It soon starts to irritate you and when you find someone else using your name, you end up giving them a slap, but that just adds to it.

The pub and nightclub security industry was starting to undergo a change. Pubs were starting to employ door-men for the first time. The door agencies were getting bigger and taking over more venues, rather than each venue employing its own door staff. This had a couple of effects. One was that the wages were kept down and the other was you would never be sure of what class of man you would be working with.

I was not keen on working for an agency even though I knew Steve Hill, who was starting to have the monopoly on providing the security to licensed premises in the Blackpool area, quite well through boxing. Steve had been a top-class professional light-heavyweight. He also had two brothers who were both very good boxers: George, who was an amateur heavyweight, and Billy, who was a professional middleweight.

The problem in my mind was not Steve, who was a top man; it was the quality of some of the doormen his agency would have to employ simply to keep up with the number of doors he was now in charge of. When you work the doors, your life can literally be in your colleagues' hands, so you need to know you can trust the men beside you.

The Blackpool club/disco scene in the early Eighties was vibrant. With its seven miles of golden sands, Blackpool stretches along the Fylde coast in a long ribbon, and clubs were dotted along the length of it, mainly concentrated in the central area between North and Central piers. On most nights of the week during the long summer season, and at weekends throughout the year, punters had the choice not just of scores of pubs and licensed hotels and guesthouses but of dozens of nightclubs, from dives like the Regency to upmarket discos like the Adam and Eve and Trader Jacks at the famous Imperial Hotel (for a partial list of the town's clubs in this period, see page seven). In their bid to attract custom, clubs constantly reinvented themselves, regularly changing names, décor and music to compete with their main rivals.

A new club opened on Topping Street, in the town centre but away from the more raucous promenade, called Secrets. It was owned and managed by Peter and Christine Schofield, who were friends of my fiancée Tanee. Peter Schofield was a well known disc jockey in the Blackpool area and he had a ready-made customer base from working at top local venues like the Adam and Eve club over the previous twenty years. He had his own following and could guarantee good local crowds. Peter and Christine did not want to use an agency and already had their head doorman sorted out, a nice guy named Geoff Manning. I had met Geoff a few times and he was only too glad to offer me a job on his team. Secrets was a huge success, opening four nights a week – Tuesday, Thursday, Friday and Saturday – and catering to a members- and locals-only market.

While at Secrets, I became good friends with Steve Warton. Steve is about five feet nine inches tall and was at that time about thirteen and a half stone in weight, a powerhouse of a man with fast hands and a huge punch capable of causing major damage. One of his favourite tricks was to stamp on his opponents' faces when he had knocked them down. I didn't say that he was nice man, I just said we became good friends.

Steve worked on the door at a club called Bunters, just off Talbot Square in the centre of Blackpool. Bunters, the club where I had knocked out the off-duty police officer, was part of a chain of clubs run by a guy named Phil Brown. Phil is originally from Liverpool and had brought some Scouse lads over to help on the Blackpool club door, big, strong men like Steve Gibbons, Jimmy Penn and Brummie. I got to know these guys really well and I still meet up with Gibbo, who now runs his own security firm in the north-west of England. Steve has looked after the door at Mr Smiths in Warrington since the mid-1980s.

Despite, or perhaps because of, the popularity of Secrets, incidents started happening there, just like they do in any other nightclub in the country. The local faces did not know me that well because I had been working the doors on the promenade, which is dominated by tourists and day-trippers, while Blackpool people tend to prefer the locals-only clubs usually situated away from the seafront. So to many I was an unknown quantity. Local hard cases tried it on with me to see how far they could push it. In the end they found out it was not very far at all.

The worst time for me when working in a pub or club is drinking-up time at the end of the night. You might not have had any trouble at all that night but at drinking-up time you can guarantee that some dick will refuse to finish until he or she is ready. One night I was trying to clear the stragglers and a man who was with a group of people was holding two pint pots of beer, one half-empty and the other one full. These were the old dimpled pint pots with handles. Luckily you don't see many of them now as they make excellent weapons that can be used against the door staff.

When I asked them to drink up for the third time, the man became argumentative and came out with the usual bollocks: 'I've paid for it, I will drink it when I am ready.' He was obviously being the big man in front of his friends. I later found out that he was their boss at a local tyre-fitting shop.

I quietly explained the drinking-up law and time to him but he wasn't having any of it.

'You don't know who you are dealing with,' he snarled.

Smiling at him, I replied, 'I am dealing with you sir, no one else.' Looking at the rest of the people in the group I could sense that they did not want to get involved. The man was about three inches shorter than me with a heavy build and his hands looked like they were used to rough work. He was becoming more aggressive and sure of himself.

I looked around to see if I could see Geoff, the head doorman, anywhere. He might know the dickhead. There was no sign of him, so it was down to me.

'Drink up now or lose them, it's that simple,' I said to him.

The guy ended up smashing one of the pint pots into the side of my head. The glass shattered and I saw stars but I didn't go down. I shook my head and blood went everywhere.

Once I see my own blood I step up a gear. I asked one of the staff to call an ambulance and then I wasted the cunt with a few good punches. I dragged him up the stairs, wasted him again and left him on the pavement outside the club. I was stood over him when the ambulance arrived. They thought they were there for me but once I had stepped out of the way they realised their mistake.

Blackpool CID attended the incident, statements were taken from witnesses confirming my story and then I was left to make my own way to the hospital, where I received half a dozen stitches in the wound. No charges were pressed against either side.

Another incident occurred when a guy named Vince Dyson was throwing his weight around against a couple of younger lads at the bar. Dyson was pally with some well-known local lads like Steve Warton, Tommy Troop (now deceased), Sean Oliver (deceased) and John Tate (deceased). He was also a bit of a local football hooligan down at Bloomfield Road and he obviously fancied his chances because when I told him to behave or he would be asked to leave, he told me to fuck off. Not having the patience I now have, I grabbed hold of him by the hair and dragged him to the door.

Once outside the club I let him go and said, 'Tell me to fuck off now.' He threw a big punch at me but missed as I twisted away from it. I returned a right cross that caught him on the point of his jaw. He went down like he had been shot in the head. The long and short of it was he ended up on a life support machine and I ended up having to keep my head down for a short while.

It was Steve Warton who came and got me out of the way. He was working with Mick Creasy at the time and Mick had spoken very highly of me. He also kept me abreast of everything that was happening. No witnesses came forward against me and luckily Vince regained his full health and did not want the police involved.

You will find people all over the country that have been in a similar position any number of times but have not been so lucky and the person that was punched has died of their injuries. This ruins lots of innocent people's lives, families and loved ones on both sides, yet it can happen in the blink of an eye.

This was in the early 1980s, when door staff were not trained or vetted like they are now. You could come out of prison and get a job on a door straight away if you could handle yourself. People did not ask questions like they have to now. In fact being an ex-con could work in your favour on some venues.

Ian Sharples and his brother Andy started working at Secrets with me. Geoff had had enough and retired, and soon Steve Warton and Sean Oliver also joined us, which made it a very nice little crew of top lads. Sean Oliver was Steve Warton's best pal. He stood about six foot four inches and, although he was not muscular, he was very big-boned. He was also a complete head-the-ball in a nice way.

One night after 1am, when Sean was on the door by himself as we were all inside the basement club, some Scottish lads who had been knocked back earlier decided to attack the door. This time they came prepared with knives, iron bars and a machete. Sean managed to press the alarm button to alert the staff in the club but received a broken arm and some cuts before we got to him. All the big brave Scots ran off as soon as they saw us coming. Sean was taken to Victoria Hospital, a frequent occurrence for Blackpool door staff (either there or the police station), frequent-flier miles not given.

Talking among ourselves after the police had left, we learned that when the Jocks had come to the door earlier they had been with a local lad nicknamed PJ. If we could not find the Jocks we could definitely find PJ, who hopefully, for his own sake, would be able to direct us to the individuals we wished to have a quiet word with.

The remaining four of us – Warton, Ian, Andy and myself – spent the next couple of hours between 3am and 5am knocking on doors. Sometimes we knocked so hard that the door fell off. At a couple of addresses we were either just in front of the police or just behind them. It was quite hairy for a while because we were obviously tooled-up and if we had been collared we would have been looking at some serious time, especially Ian due to his past record.

We were finally given an address in a block of flats on the corner of Springfield Road and the promenade. We arrived and forced our way into a flat to find PJ throwing items of furniture through the window to try to attract help. PJ finally gave us an address on Rydal Avenue, just off Central Drive, where the Scots cunts were renting a house.

We decided to act like the police making an early morning raid; that way the neighbours might not phone the Old Bill at all, but if they did we might have enough time to get our message across. We did not have mobile phones in those days so we had to synchronise our watches and hit the front and back doors simultaneously. We were tooled-up to fuck because we knew they were and they had already proved that they were willing to use their weapons when they had assaulted Sean.

We crashed through the doors and ran into the house. Those that came through the back door covered the ground floor while the front door crew went straight up the stairs. Our adrenalin was pumping, not knowing who or what was waiting for us. Anyone who has done this type of thing themselves will know the thrill or buzz that goes through you. Even when you see trained police officers doing it on the television news you can see how psyched up they are.

The only problem was that they had already left; they had packed up and fucked off, the cupboards were bare. In the end it was down to the police to find and prosecute them. It just shows, they are useful for some things.

7

Branching Out

NEW NIGHTCLUBS WERE opening in Blackpool all the time as the town changed its focus from traditional family fun to a more youth-oriented, alcohol-driven night-time economy. The phrase 'lager lout' had not yet been coined but we already had them by the thousand. One of the new clubs, just around the corner from Secrets near the town's main bus station on Talbot Road, was Just Ji's. Another was down on Central Drive called the Village. Steve Warton left Secrets to go to the Village as the head doorman, which was a very good move for him. Rumours started about Secrets being sold to a woman who styled herself 'Lady Rachel' and who was supposedly worth millions of pounds. Peter and Christine Schofield, the owners, both denied it right to the end. Finally, on the day that the sale went through, Peter gathered the security team around him and told us the news.

'What is going to happen to us, is she keeping us on?' I asked him.

He looked at me and said, 'I don't know and I don't really care now that the sale has gone through.'

That was when I hit him, just the once. That was all it needed. It took a long time before I even acknowledged him again.

Things did not work out between the security staff and the woman who called herself Lady Rachel. We parted company one night after she had slapped me around the face because I called her a fraud, a liar and a cheat. And she was: she ended up being sent to prison.

They put a new door team on at the club the next evening. These lads tried to keep us out but we were owed wages and they would have got hurt if they had tried too hard – and they knew it. While we waited we helped ourselves to drinks. I know this was a bit naughty but we had to prove a point. Lady Rachel and her male friend, if you could call him a man, ended up phoning the police on us. A large contingent of Blackpool's finest, the proper boys in the blue overalls, came to escort us from the premises but only after we had received our money.

Steve Warton asked me to join his team of lads at the Village. Ian Sharples went to the new club, Just Ji's, around the corner from Secrets by the main bus station. Ian and I had both been to see the owners, Stan and Sheila, as the club was being refurbished but at that time they were convinced that they were okay with the team that they had in place. Things didn't go as well as expected with the men they hired and so two weeks later they got in touch with Ian. Both doors were run as private concerns. It always works better that way on locals' clubs, the customers soon get to know the regular team and vice versa.

The Village, where I joined Steve Warton, was an old cinema that was converted to a nightclub and restaurant around 1985. It held about eight hundred people upstairs with a nice Italian restaurant on the ground floor. We had a good strong team on the Village but even so we had some funny incidents there.

It was a Saturday night in the summer season, about 1am. I was sat in the restaurant with a police inspector, who was taking a statement from me about an incident that had occurred at the front entrance the night before. Steve Warton approached us and asked the inspector if he could spare me for a few minutes. The inspector was quite happy to sit there with a cup of coffee as it was pouring down with rain outside. It turned out that one of Steve's friends, a lad from Liverpool called Ian, had just been jumped by a big group of lads on Central Drive after they had walked in front of his car, nearly causing an accident. He had come to the club to ask for some help.

Four of us piled into Ian's BMW with him and shot off in the direction these lads had taken.

'That's them,' he said, pointing out a group of about ten lads walking down the street in the rain.

We parked further up the drive and casually got out of Scouse Ian's car. The group of lads had just about reached us when one of them recognised either Ian or his car.

We hit them with the same effect as a ten-pin bowling ball hits the skittles. They went all over the place. One of them crashed straight through a shop window, setting off the burglar alarms, and as Central Drive is a busy road we were soon attracting a lot of attention. We split up and made our way back to the club on foot.

I re-entered the downstairs restaurant to rejoin the police inspector. He took in my soaking clothes, wet hair and bloody knuckles. He closed his eyes, shook his head and said, 'I don't think I want to know, do I?'

It was around this time that I made my first Crown Court appearance, for grievous bodily harm. I had been to the magistrates' courts on numerous counts by now but, sticking to my dad's advice and a large amount of good luck, had kept my record clear, except for the Isle of Wight incident.

Now Crown Court is a whole different ball game to the magistrates', as I was to find out. To end up there, the charge against you had to be of a more serious nature where they could hand out more severe sentences, or you as a defendant could request trial by jury if you believed it to be in your best interest. The courts no longer allow the defendant to choose this second option.

I was accused of hitting a man and breaking his cheekbone to the extent that he needed plastic surgery. This was an incident at the Village where six men had been thrown out of the club for fighting. I was on the VIP entrance at the other side of the club by myself. As they walked by, they decided to have a go at me. This was before door staff had radios, so I was incommunicado. The first one to get close took a big right hand and that was enough to make the others think again. One hour later the police arrived to question me. They then arrested me for assault.

By the time I was to appear at Blackpool Magistrates' Court, the charge against me had been raised to GBH and I was to be sent to Crown Court at Preston. As I said earlier Crown Court is a whole different ball game. It is a lot scarier than the lower court, the barristers are in their silks (wigs and gowns) with the solicitors behind them, then there are the twelve jurors eyeballing you and believing everything the prosecution is saying about you. It is nothing like on television, where you see the defence objecting all the time.

I was very lucky in that I got a fair hearing and a not guilty verdict on the grounds of self defence. It might have helped that the man I had hit was a TV licence inspector. However, this seemed to be the start of something between me and the Blackpool police. Every time I got arrested from then on, the police seemed to up the charge where possible. Whether this was tactics on their part to try to make me plead down to a lesser charge or just that they wanted to stick it up me as far as it would go, I don't know. Maybe someone at the police station had a bit of foresight into what was to come or they were just being bloody-minded.

Not long after this, an off-duty copper managed to get himself a good hiding in the club. I chased the attacker out of the club and returned to help the injured cop. With him being unconscious, I applied the emergency first aid that all local doormen had been taught during 'door safe' training, a local council and police initiative that made sure that door staff knew the basic 'Dr ABC' emergency procedures, i.e. danger, airways, breathing and circulation. After making sure he was okay, I then called an ambulance.

Another off-duty copper came looking for his pal, found him in a prostrate condition and started having a go at me. Now this cunt was a big rugby player so things got a bit heated for a while. The next thing, uniformed police turned up and I was arrested on suspicion of GBH on the unconscious copper. I was taken to Blackpool nick, stripped of all my clothes for forensics except for my socks and underwear and thrown in a cell. I asked for a lawyer straight away so that I could get my head down for the night without the police questioning me whenever they liked.

I was fast asleep in the cell when the door was thrown open and in walked the duty sergeant and two other big coppers.

'Get up Sinclair. We want to know what happened to our colleague and you are going to tell us, now.'

Sitting up, I reached down and pulled off my socks one at a time, whilst maintaining eye contact with the sergeant.

'What are you doing?' the sergeant asked me.

I stood up and said, 'If I am going to be dancing about with you three I don't intend to be slipping all over the place because I have my socks on.'

This held them in check for a few seconds until I also said, 'Before you do anything, I suggest you ask your injured pal if I had anything to do with him being where he is, because if we go any further here, you will all be very sorry in the near future.' Thankfully they backed off until the injured copper had a chance to confirm that I had not been involved in his assault. This also cleared the air between me and his rugby pal that I had got into it with.

I ended up getting released at about 5pm the next afternoon in a paper suit and a pair of paper shoes because my clothes were still at the forensic laboratory. If you know where the Blackpool police station is, you will know how busy that area can be, especially at that time of day. Who said that the police don't have a sense of humour? The twats.

The head of Blackpool Police at that time, a Super-intendent Mackay, was now starting to take an interest in my name. We had not yet met personally but we would in the near future.

My best pal, Ian Sharples, was now the head doorman at Just Ji's. I was still working at the Village, which was approximately a mile away. One Thursday night I had a visitor telling me that Ian had been taken to hospital after an incident on the door at Just Ji's. The other lads that I worked with offered to cover for me if I wanted to get off, so I jumped into my car and headed to the club to find out what had happened. Sure enough there had been a problem with a large group of blokes on a works night out. Ian had blocked them from entering the club and they had kicked off. In the rumpus that followed, Ian had sustained a nasty cut under his right eye that would need stitches.

I found Ian at the Victoria Hospital accident and emergency unit. His eye was a bloody mess and he was not a happy bunny. The cut had required about twenty stitches and whoever had done the stitching had not done it very well, as Ian's eye was pulled down at the corner. We ended up staying awake all night to find out who was responsible. It turned out they were a group of men on a works night out from a company called Taylor and Hyde, which specialised in making mirrors and had a factory about half a mile from the town centre.

At 7am that day, Ian, his brother Andrew and I were parked about twenty yards away from Taylor and Hyde's warehouse. We sat and watched as the workforce arrived, waiting until Ian recognised the main culprit, with whom he wished to have a special word. The body upon which we had been waiting finally arrived and entered the premises. As we were about to leave our car, the main shutters opened and a wagon began to reverse out of the warehouse. Ian said that the driver was one of the men from last night, so as the wagon stopped Andy opened its door and dragged out the driver. Ian and I then ran into the warehouse. We were both carrying baseball bats. We caught the main group involved in the previous night's entertainment and scattered them. Ian went straight for the big man that he believed was responsible for his injury while I backed up the others by giving a couple of them a quick introduction to my Louisville slugger. I was soon joined by Andy, who had let the driver go after giving him a quick slap or two.

Ian had put the big cunt down and was reminding him about the previous night. There was shit and all sorts coming out of the man's overalls. We explained to them that if they brought trouble to where we work, we would bring it straight back to them.

When we got back into the car to leave, we nearly kicked Ian out: he had human shit all over his shoes from the dirty bastard he had banged and it stank to high heaven.

The Taylor and Hyde office staff had rung the police, having thought the place was about to be robbed. They investigated the incident and questioned Ian but in the end no charges were pressed against anyone, including those responsible for the damage to Ian's eye.

The Village was at that time the premier club in town for the locals. The promenade was the place for the holidaymakers with popular clubs like Sands and the giant Palace nitespot. That didn't necessarily mean the Village was an easier door to work, however. One night I was on the VIP door, by myself again, when one of the waiters from the restaurant came through and told me that it had just gone bang off on the main door. It turned out that four blokes had been knocked back and they had decided to have a go with the doormen instead of just walking away. They had given a right good account of themselves before they fucked off.

When I got the chance I went over to the main door to see what had happened. The lads looked like they had been in a war. When I say 'lads' I mean Steve Warton, Tommy Throup and a couple of others, all top boys. They had been taken by surprise. The four blokes, one of whom was about six feet eight inches tall and built like a block of flats, had just piled into them. The only one of the team who seemed unmarked was Steve Warton. I was told that he had stamped his man, which, as I have mentioned, was one of Steve's favourite tricks: once he knocked someone down, he would dig his heel into the unfortunate person's head or body with considerable force.

Pulling Steve to one side, I asked him if he had indeed stamped his man.

'Yes,' he replied.

'Properly stamped him?'

'Yes.'

'Then he will have to go to the hospital, won't he?' I said smiling.

I saw the light go on in Steve's eyes. 'Fucking hell,

yes.' He was nearly jumping with joy.

Victoria Hospital was only about two miles from the club, so Steve and I jumped into his car and shot up to it. Parking his car out of the way, we walked towards the accident and emergency entrance.

You might ask, why go to these lengths, is it a revenge thing? I have always looked at it like this: if they walk away laughing, thinking that they have turned you over, they will tell everyone they know about it and then, before you know it, other groups might start trying the same thing. But if you go and change the result they can tell who they fucking want then.

We were thirty yards away when three men walked out through the doors. Straight away Steve Warton said, 'This is them.' The fourth man had obviously been kept in for treatment.

Looking at them approaching, I said to Steve, 'You take those two and I will take the big one.' Saying nothing and going straight in would give us the surprise this time. It was over in thirty seconds or less, with all three down on the floor. Before Steve could do his party trick the taxi drivers nearby started shouting and hollering that they had radioed for the police.

We had achieved our goal, two of us had turned them over, so we turned and legged it in the opposite direction. Not wanting to get his car in case the taxi drivers took the registration number, Steve went to a phone booth and rang Christine, his girlfriend at that time, who was the manageress of the Village. He asked her to come for us and told her where we were waiting.

She only turned up in her Toyota MR2 sports car, a two-seater, and then she only wanted to take Steve; but he insisted that it was both of us. In the end I had to sit on Warton's lap with my head sticking out of the sun roof all the way back to the club. It was like a ride on the Pleasure Beach.

In September 1988, Michael Jackson was booked to perform at Aintree in Liverpool. At that time, Jackson was
the biggest thing in pop, and his Bad World Tour was
his first as a solo artist. He ended up performing 123
concerts over four continents, in front of 4.4 million
people. That gives you an idea of what a phenomenon
he was at the time.

And with one hundred and twenty-five thousand
people expected to attend the Liverpool show, it was
to be the biggest single concert of the entire tour. The
security requirements were so extensive that the security
managers had to subcontract to firms from as far afield
as London. Gibbo, a pal of ours from Liverpool who
ran his own security business, asked us if we could put
a team together to work at the show under his company
name of Protectatec.

About ten of us travelled over on the day of the concert, including Steve Warton, John Tate, Les Fishwick
and myself. We arrived nice and early and met up with
Gibbo and his mates for a bit of lunch at the Pen and
Wig, a public house run by the lads. We were introduced
to Gary Spiers, who was the main security contractor
for the Liverpool men. Gary was a huge brute of a man
from New Zealand. He wore sandals all the time because
his feet were too big for shoes. He was a martial arts
legend who had learned karate in the brutal dojos of
Japan and then came to England, where he taught in
gyms and worked on the doors. Gary was famous for
taking apart entire gangs on his own. Although I did
not get to know him well, everyone I met who knew
him respected him.

When we arrived at Aintree Racecourse, we were told
that we were not to wear jackets or coats, otherwise no

one would be able to see our identifying security T-shirts. But it wasn't that warm. Gibbo had a large box full of T-shirts with his security firm logo on the front and back and I ended up putting about ten of these shirts on. I didn't intend freezing my nuts off for anyone, especially not for Michael Jackson.

Our group was put in charge of backstage security which was a bit of a result for us. Kim Wilde, who was a supporting artist, was very friendly but I think we were all a bit too old for Michael Jackson's taste.

To put this into perspective, Jackson at that time was the biggest megastar in the music world and one of the most recognisable human beings on the planet, and all he really had looking after him were a bunch of doormen from Liverpool and Blackpool.

The entire area was cordoned of by a fence that was approximately eight or nine feet high. There were plenty of people outside trying to get in without tickets, this was Liverpool after all. During our break periods we would go for a walk and check out the crowd. Sometimes we would come across people climbing the fences or selling drugs but what the hell, our job was to look after the backstage area. We were equipped with radios and went out in pairs so it was not too bad and we managed to have a laugh or two. By the time I made my way backstage again I was freezing: I had sold all my extra security shirts in exchange for a small fortune. You don't have to be a Scouser to do a shady deal.

Through the course of the afternoon and evening there were a few attempts to storm the fences by people outside without tickets (or security shirts), but let me tell you something, when we saw the other security firms turning up, it looked like someone had emptied every Category A prison in the country and asked them to work the Jackson concert. There were more broken noses and scarred faces in one place than I had ever seen before. Yet everything was contained and managed well considering there were so many different firms working in one area. That showed the respect that people had for Gary Spiers. Probably no-one else could have brought those men together. It also made me realise how powerful door-men could be if they worked together. I had already seen with the football hooligans how, if you have fifty lads who will stand together and fight, you have a formidable force, even if individually they were not much. Imagine what you could do with fifty doormen all together?

8

Casualty

IT WAS A beautiful midsummer Sunday and I was about twenty-eight years of age. Tanee had gone down to Cornwall with her mum Norma for a week's break. The weather was wonderful and I was on the loose with Sharpie and some of the lads. It was Poulton Club Day, a charity event arranged for certain areas or venues that is staged every summer in Poulton-le-Fylde, a small town near Blackpool. There were beer tents and game stalls set out in a field to raise cash for local good causes. From there we moved on to a man named Ken Speed's house. There was a fair group of us who knew each other well and also people we did not know, but everyone was getting on well though and the drink and nosebag was flowing freely.

I wandered outside with my drink with a couple of lads, one that I worked the doors with called Glen Lawson and a pal of his. Shortly after, the people inside the house heard the screech of brakes and the sickening thud of an impact. A car had hit me. I was thrown forward onto the bonnet, smashing the headlight and indicator and continuing into the windscreen to end up in a somersault over the roof. Then I smashed head-first onto the road.

I recovered consciousness to find my mate Ian cradling my head in his lap, with tears streaming down his face and some bird from the party checking for a pulse (I didn't know you could find a pulse down there). Turns out she was a nurse and she was checking to see if there were any breaks around my pelvic area. My jeans were torn from the impact and there was a gash on my left thigh. My head was a mass of blood and I felt like I had been hit by a bus.

Typically the cops showed up before the ambulance arrived and started asking questions. One of the girls from the party said to the officer, 'It was a blue Ford that hit him, it went that way,' pointing down the lane. I was still lying in the middle of the road in pain but I quickly contradicted her and said to the officer, 'No it was a red car, possibly a Citroen.'

The girl looked at me as if I was crazy.

'It was a blue Ford,' she said again.

'It fucking hit me,' I snarled at her, 'I should know what colour it was.'

One of the lads steered her away just as the ambulance arrived, causing the questioning to be put on hold for a while.

I was pretty banged up and on crutches afterwards but I did not want to let Tanee know about it in case it ruined her holiday. At the time I was to be the manager of a new club that was to open on Blackpool Promenade called Lips. It caused me a fair bit of pain and discomfort but we still opened on time.

When the police came to the club a few weeks later to interview me, Sharpie was there keeping me company and having a few drinks.

'It has come to our attention that you know who it was who hit you with the car and you will sort it out yourself,' the copper said.

He left in a huff when we started laughing, thinking we were laughing at him. What they did not know was that Sharpie had left the party for some reason, to buy more booze or nosebag, whatever. I was stood outside with Glen and his mate, having a quiet drink when he came back. Seeing us standing in the lane, he put the pedal to the metal, thinking we would all jump clear and get out of the way. Glen and the other lad did but I thought, *he will stop*. Sharpie, in turn, thought, *he will jump clear.*

Well he didn't stop and I didn't jump.

They say that your life flashes in front of you in a situation like this but all I can remember seeing was the look of horror on Sharpie's face and thinking, *oh shit.*

Still, no harm done in the end.

Lips nightclub was on the Blackpool Golden Mile close to the Foxhall public house. I had been asked to manage it by the Stefani family, who owned the pier at Fleetwood and the Village nightclub on Central Drive, where I was working at the time, amongst other properties. The club catered for approximately three hundred people and was based underneath a hotel owned by the same family. When I was asked by the Stefanis if I would do the job and I accepted, I was informed that the security for the club would be provided by Stephen Hill. Steve ran a door security agency in the town and I had known him for about ten years. At the time I was not too happy about having an agency on the door. I had always worked private doors, that way you knew who you would be working with, whereas with an agency anyone could turn up.

I agreed on one condition, that I could have some-one of my choosing to watch my back. The Stefanis accepted my terms and I hired one of my friends: Ian Crawford. Ian, better known in Blackpool as 'Crowie', was a shaven-headed figure who was well-known on the town's doors. He stands about five feet ten and weighed about twelve and a half stone at the time. Crowie is a few years older than me and was known as a hard case.

He always carried a tool and he was not afraid to use it and was working for Brian London at the 007 club when I first met him.

I also had another pal of mine working with us as the club cellarman and DJ. This was a lad from Middlesbrough called Jimmy Telford, better known as Jimmy the Dancer. He had got his nickname after coming second or third in a national disco dancing competition. The first time I met Jimmy was when I had been asked to clear up a misunderstanding over some outstanding rent. I went to an address in Blackpool that I had been given, which turned out to be a basement flat. I found a man of about five feet ten inches and twelve stone with long curly blond hair who spoke with what sounded like a Geordie accent. He was out in the yard, in the process of trying to saw the sharp edge off an axe. I stood and watched him for a few minutes and then asked him what he was doing.

'I'm having a bit of bother with my landlord and he's threatened that he's going to send some heavies down to sort me out.'

'So why are you sawing off the blade of the axe?' I asked him.

'Well I don't want to kill anyone,' he said, smiling.

Walking down the steps, I asked him to let me have a look at the axe. He handed it over to me. It was still nowhere near sawn through. Holding the axe in my hands, I looked him in the eyes and then introduced myself.

'Fucking hell,' he said, and rolled his eyes in disgust. I couldn't help but like the guy, and we sorted out his debt amicably. We still laugh about it now.

We had some right battles in Lips and Jimmy probably caused most of them, but he was such a laugh to have around and he could turn his hand to most things. One night I was stood on the door talking to Crowie when I heard this scream from down in the club. The doors

ERROR

at the bottom of the stairs flew open and Dancer come flying up them as if his arse was on fire. Behind him was one of the biggest men I had ever seen and he was being followed by his friends. What the fuck has he done now, I asked myself. It turned out that he had said or implied something to the big man's girlfriend and the giant had taken exception to it. I tried reasoning with him but in the end it went bang off and we had to do the business, which as luck would have it we managed to do.

Another time, Jimmy called me to a domestic kicking off on the dance floor between two couples. When I intervened I was met with a torrent of abuse from both parties. I got a bit annoyed myself and I said to the two blokes involved, 'If you two don't sort these women out then I will knock you out myself.' Well that went down like a lead balloon and shortly after so did the two blokes. The next thing I knew I was struggling like a lunatic with these two birds, who were trying to rip off my face. Turning around, I looked for some help from the Dancer. Guess what that clown was doing? He was only kneeling down checking to see what type of watches or jewellery the two guys I'd knocked out were wearing. He had plenty of faults but his loyalty made up for it.

The club being on the promenade, it catered mainly to holidaymakers and day-trippers, so when the season ended at the beginning of November, Lips closed down for the winter and I returned to the Village. Although I was back among a good team of lads, I wasn't settled just being one of the boys. It was in my mind now that I had the experience and was capable of running a pub or a club. I had left school with no qualifications at all and my only ambitions then had been to travel the world, but now I could see other opportunities opening up for me.

Just Ji's on Talbot Road in the centre of Blackpool was at the time a top local venue.

My friend Ian Sharples had been running the door there for Stan and Sheila, the owners, but had left to manage his own club, the Adam and Eve on Chapel Street. Ian had recommended me to the owners of the club to take over from him when he left. Stan and Sheila were a lovely couple from Yorkshire who were only too happy to agree to this, as they both knew me quite well by then through me visiting Ian when he had been working for them and also when we had sorted out a few problems such as the Taylor and Hyde firm.

I started on the Thursday night the week before my thirtieth birthday. The first night passed without anything exciting happening but, unbeknown to me, there had been an incident the previous week between some local scallies and a couple of coloured lads from Preston. By all accounts the local lads had taken a bit of a liberty and, heavily outnumbering the Preston lads, had given them a slap.

Now these lads must have been well thought of back home in Preston because the following week, and my second night at Just Ji's, a group of about twenty of them turned up at the club's front door looking for revenge. I was quickly informed about the previous week's episode and took the decision to block them from entering the club. After a heated discussion, to put it mildly, punches and kicks were aimed at us and so we closed the doors on them.

The doors were big see-through safety glass and we could clearly see the lads outside getting more and more agitated. Just then, four white lads tried making their way through the Preston lads to the club door. All of a sudden it went bang off. The four lads didn't have a clue what hit them. I stood watching for a few seconds, weighing up the odds: new job, be sensible, keep the door shut and call the police, or go out and help the four lads.

Fuck. All four white lads were down and taking a proper kicking. *Fuck. Fuck. Fuck.*

Never being one to take the sensible route, I shouted, 'Let's have it,' and unlocked and opened the door. Four of us jumped out of the club and into the affray, causing the group from Preston to disperse. However, when they saw there were only a few of us, they quickly regrouped and came back at us in force.

In those days, conflict management was unheard of and to be truthful I could not really see it having much effect if I held up my open palms and presented a non-aggressive stance whilst standing slightly to the side. It was like a scene from Rorke's Drift, the battle that the film *Zulu* was based on. I went past the four white lads, who were all down on the floor, trying to give others the chance to help them up and into the club. But I was quickly surrounded and found myself struggling.

I kept hearing shouts of, 'Do the white cunt.'

I was managing to block most of the punches that were being thrown at me and luckily for me they were getting in each other's way. I butted, punched and kicked like Jackie Chan but they just kept coming. Stepping forward, I managed to drop one of the bastards with a big right and took the opportunity to get away by bulling myself through the opening I had created in their ranks.

I knew I was hurt. All my strength had left me and my legs were wobbling but I couldn't understand why. There was no pain and I hadn't taken any big shots to my head although I had been surrounded by about eight of the twats. I managed to get across the road and leaned against a chemist shop window. I was fucked. Two of them were coming at me now from across the road, both big bastards. I pushed myself upright from the shop front to meet them but I had nothing left in me. A figure flew past me from behind, smashing into my would-be assailants, taking them away from me. Others came running from the entrance of the club. With the numbers starting to equalise, the group of Preston lads decided to leave the immediate vicinity at the double; in other words, they fucked off quick.

'Steve! Steve! Are you okay mate?'

Alan McNeal, a good mate of mine who also worked the doors, had turned back to me after seeing off the two big bastards.

'You're bleeding all over the place,' he said.

Lifting my suit jacket, I became aware of blood spurting from just beneath my left ribcage. I had not felt a thing. It just goes to show how much effect an adrenalin rush can have upon your body.

My left trouser leg was already being soaked red. I was losing blood and losing it fast. I had not felt too bad until then, but once you see your own blood pumping out of you like that you slip into what is known as an 'emotional mindset'. My legs, which had already been weak, suddenly went weaker; forcing me to lean on Steve Swallow, another doorman who had also come to my assistance. I might have even started to get a bit of religion, you know what I mean, oh God please don't let me die, I promise I will change my life if you give me another chance, all that bollocks. Even then, I think I had my fingers crossed.

Looking around it was like a battlefield. The white lads who had been attacked for no other reason than being in the wrong place at the wrong time were all still down. I did not know it then but two of them had also been stabbed.

There was no time to waste, so one of my pals jumped in front of a taxi that was driving past to make sure it stopped. The driver, whose nickname, believe it or not, was 'Zulu' (although he was white), knew me and had no hesitation in telling me to get in even though there was claret leaking out of me and going everywhere. We made Victoria Hospital in record time. 'Zulu' drove the taxi right into the accident and emergency ambulance parking space. Blackpool on a Friday night in August can be quite rowdy so at that time there was a queue of two or three people already waiting to be processed. Holding my elbow over my jacket and applying pressure with my arm was being quite effective in stopping the bleeding, so I patiently joined the queue.

When my turn came the lady on the desk already had the form in front of her.

'Name?'

'Stephen Sinclair.'

'Address?'

'Elizabeth Street, Blackpool.'

'Doctor's name and surgery address, please?' And so on.

'Right and what seems to be the problem, Mr Sinclair?' she asked with a quizzical look.

'I have been stabbed,' I replied.

'Where?' she asked, writing my answers onto the form.

Moving my arm away and lifting my jacket, I said, 'Here.' Blood came pouring out, causing the poor lady to jump up in a panic and start shouting for assistance and asking me why I hadn't said anything sooner.

I was placed on to a trolley and wheeled into a treatment room, where I was attended to by a staff nurse or matron. Peeling my blood-soaked shirt away from my body, she exposed a small stab wound of about two centimetres in length. It was just under my left ribcage with blood seeping out. Using a large dressing, she calmly applied pressure to the wound until the bleeding stopped. Still talking calmly to me, telling me that everything looked okay, the nurse turned to throw the bloody dressing she had used to stem the bleeding into a waste receptacle. Just then Tanee turned up. She had been contacted at the Village, where she then worked and which I had only left the week before, by some of my pals who had been with me.

After throwing herself on me for a big cuddle and a quick tear or two, she began asking the nurse some questions. As they were talking, I happened to notice that my stomach and side around the stab wound had started to swell considerably.

'Excuse me sister, is this normal?' I asked.

The nurse, being very experienced, took one look at me and grabbed the phone. She identified herself and asked for an emergency operating theatre.

'I repeat, an emergency operating theatre. We have a patient with a stab wound to the left side upper abdomen that has internal bleeding.'

This brought a fresh flow of tears from Tanee – okay, and possibly a few from me! Anyway, the next minute I was being whisked off on the trolley and being prepped for an emergency operation.

It is a very strange feeling when you are being wheeled away down a hospital corridor from someone you love, thinking that you may die, but it must have been worse for Tanee watching me being rushed off and knowing that she might lose me.

The next morning, when I came to after the operation, all of the nursing staff on the ward were being very curt and off with me. As far as they were concerned, I had been involved in a mass knife fight where up to five people, including me, had been stabbed. It was only when the *Blackpool Gazette* came out later that day, naming me as a Good Samaritan and saying that I had 'gone to the aid of two youths fleeing a thirty-strong mob', that the attitude of the hospital staff changed towards me.

I spent ten days in hospital recovering from the wound after an infection set in. The surgeon who had carried out the operation told me how lucky I had been not to be killed. If the weapon had travelled upwards it could have pierced my heart. The other lads stabbed were all okay in that their wounds were not life-threatening and they were given early release from the hospital.

I spent my thirtieth birthday laid up in hospital with drips and tubes going into and coming out of different parts of my body. The visitors I received caused the nursing staff some concern though. Most of them looked like they had escaped from prison and they were trying to sneak alcohol, drugs and wank mags in to me all the time.

The Blackpool police had actually stopped three cars that were heading back to Preston full of the lads that had been involved in the incident. They were all questioned back at the Blackpool police station but no arrests were made at that time. When the local CID interviewed me in my hospital bed, they told me about the uniformed police stopping the cars and questioning the group from Preston but said no weapons were found. Now I knew these officers quite well and they seemed a bit put out about this. They then told me that the Preston police had informed them that they could not assist the Blackpool police because this group lived on a certain estate in a 'no-go area of Preston'. What the fuck was that all about? This was Preston we were talking about, not fucking Baghdad.

From another friendly police source, I obtained the name and the occupation of a certain individual who they believed was responsible for my stabbing, but was told to keep it to myself. On my release from hospital, the police had no further leads and their investigation seemed to be coming to a standstill. The only other piece of information I had received was that the suspect drank in a pub called the Red Lion on Church Street in the centre of Preston. This pub was frequented predominantly by blacks and again I had been warned it was a no-go area for the Preston CID. Fucking good job I was not in the Preston CID, eh?

I had received plenty of visitors whilst I was in hospital, lads that I worked with on the doors and others that were just up for a bit of retaliation. Once I had recovered enough to get around a bit, I started to make some plans. I got together with a couple of good pals, one of whom is now dead, John Tate. John was a top bloke who was well up for it, whatever it was. We had both served in the Royal Engineers although in different squadrons. I will call the other one Steve; again he was another top lad up for anything. We discussed how, what, where and when, making changes if someone came up with a better idea.

I did not want to make the same mistake as the lads from Preston had. The more people that were involved, the less control you have on the situation. We had borrowed a car from one of the lads who dabbled as a car dealer; the car was not registered in his name, so if anything did happen, it would take the police some time to trace it.

Tooled up with our favourite equalisers – mine being a sawn-off pump-action shotgun – we drove over to Preston. We had previously worked out the best place to park the car and a plan of action. I intended to shoot the cunt in the legs.

We walked through the front door of the Red Lion into a small room of about twenty foot square with no-one in it, not even a member of the bar staff. When a barmaid did finally appear we ordered our drinks and I asked politely, 'Where is everyone tonight?'

'Everyone is in the back room,' she said, pointing to a door at the rear.

My heart was pounding in my chest, my mouth had gone dry and my sphincter muscle had developed a twitch. Looking at the other two, I could see they were both feeling the same as me. I smiled and moved towards the door that the barmaid had pointed to. We walked through a corridor into a very dark long room with another bar immediately to our right. It took a minute for our eyes to adjust; the room was thick with marijuana smoke. When I could finally see, it took a bit of an effort to stop my bottom jaw dropping. The place was packed with people smoking ganja. There must have been more than a hundred black men and women in there and they were all looking directly at us.

Funny how your plans can change at such short notice, eh? Obviously we left because we did not want innocent people to get hurt.

Outside the premises we were confronted by a very aggressive male who wanted some form of confrontation. He put himself in my face, threatening me with all sorts of violence. I calmly explained that he had the wrong person and he definitely had the wrong time. He continued to push and push right up to me pulling my coat open, at which he suddenly agreed that he did have the wrong person, he was very sorry and he was going to go away now, if that was okay with me.

Another time, I actually fronted an individual at his workplace, just to let him know that I knew who he was and where he worked. He went white and started getting very excited, saying he had had nothing to do with it. I just stared straight into his eyes, smiled and told him that I would see him again soon. Then I walked away.

That night when we returned to Blackpool, I retrieved my car and made my way home. As soon as I pulled up outside my house, the Blackpool police were all over me. The individual in question had been onto the Preston police, who had then contacted their Blackpool colleagues. I was very fortunate that we had stashed our tools and that I was not carrying anything at that time, either in the car or on me.

You have to remember that as far as I was concerned this man had tried to kill me. You don't stab someone under the ribs if you are just intending to wound or hurt them.

It took me quite a long time and some pretty hairy moments, with a few doors going through, sometimes the wrong ones, but I did finally manage to get some closure on the incident when my alleged assailant was himself the victim of a serious accident.

One of the most disconcerting things about the whole incident was that the week after I was stabbed, two black men that were not known to the security staff tried to enter Just Ji's. They were refused entry for their own safety. Local feelings were still very agitated and the lads on the door really feared for their safety if they were allowed into the club. These two men took the owners of the club, Stan and Sheila, to court and were awarded £2,500 each for having their feelings hurt. I wish someone would hurt my feelings like that.

A few weeks later I was back in the gym at the Commonwealth Club on Central Drive, trying to get myself back in shape. I did a fair bit of running and some bag and pad work with plenty of sit-ups to strengthen my stomach. I was approached by a man called Joey Jones, who I learned was a boxing trainer. He knew that I had done some boxing in the past and so he asked me if I would do a bit of sparring with a young heavyweight from the north-east.

I thought about it for a couple of seconds and then said, 'Why not.' That's how I met and became friends with big Dave Garside from Hartlepool.

Dave made a big impression in Blackpool. He set up his own security company with my friend Steve Daley and another lad called Alan Levene, a good pro fighter from Liverpool. Although their company managed to get a couple of lucrative local contracts, the Blackpool police were all over them and in the end they had to close it down. Dave went on to marry Melanie Harper, the daughter of ex-boxing champ Brian London. They now have their own family and live back up in the north-east of England where they are very successful with their own security company.

Dave is also into boxing promotions in quite a big way. He used to invite me up to Hartlepool every now and again and we would also go over to Liverpool for boxing evenings or sometimes just for an evening out. Respect to you, big guy.

9

Public Enemy

SAMUEL COLT NICKNAMED it 'the equaliser' and it made all men equal, whatever their size or strength. Gun culture is rife in this country, no matter what the police or Government say. In Blackpool alone I could tell you of thirty or more people that I knew for a fact, at one time or another, had possession of one or more guns, be they handguns, sawn-off shotguns or even semi-automatic weapons. The difference between the people in Blackpool and other areas such as Liverpool or Manchester is that we have a better quality of life. We generally have more to lose than some of the criminal types in the big cities, especially the younger element who will do anything to impress and gain street cred. They love the gangster image, the respect they get from their peers. Me, I just wanted to make a few bob and keep below the police radar.

I was getting a lot of propositions asking me to collect outstanding debts or provide muscle or protection to certain elements, both local and out of town. A couple of times it nearly came bang on top for me because I was not carrying anything, so I decided to get myself a small handgun that would be easy to conceal. I had received small arms weapon training in the army so I knew they were not toys and that you should never play the fool with them. If you pull it out you must be willing to use it. A shooter is no use to anyone if you are only trying to scare someone and are not willing to squeeze the trigger. Indeed you are better off not letting anyone know that you are carrying until you need it.

I knew that Tanee was the right girl for me when I was arrested again for some alleged offence. The police had a warrant to search the flat that we were living in on Raikes Parade. It was late at night and I was being held in custody. Tanee's stepmother, Norma, was visiting with us for a few days from Oldham. Asking the police if she could just wake Norma first before they trampled the place, Tanee took the opportunity to hide my little peacemaker in the dog's bean bag and got Norma to keep the dog, Sammy, a Yorkshire terrier, sat on it while the police searched the rest of the flat. Although she was not happy about it she still did it for me. You can't ask for more than that. Thanks love.

The first gun I ever owned was an old World War Two officer's Webley revolver. It was a monster in size and if I remember rightly it fired a .45 calibre bullet, which is huge. Since then I have seen automatic weapons and pump-action shotguns passing through certain hands in Blackpool.

The trouble with young lads who have received no firearms training getting their hands on guns is that they want to fire them and once they have fired them they start to want to shoot something or someone. I must just say this now for legal reasons, I handed all my guns in during the amnesty appeals by the north-west police forces. Oh yes.

A quiet lie-in was ruined by a loud smashing noise downstairs. I was arrested at home at about seven o'clock in the morning by uniformed police and CID officers coming through the front and back doors simultaneously. I was taken away in handcuffs for questioning on an alleged contract hit.

I had a fear that I was being set up. Apparently the police had received an anonymous telephone call naming me as the assailant when a man had been badly beaten. I was thrown into a cold, dirty police cell in the Lytham police station. I didn't know it then but I would be there for a few days. I asked for a solicitor straight away and so managed to get a few hours of rest until he turned up. Luckily for me the police investigation failed to make any type of case against me, but they tried; boy, did they try.

The police had arrested another man, called Graham Blow, on suspicion of being involved in this crime and accused him of paying me to do the job, but again there was no evidence against him and so he was also released from custody. We had not previously known each other but it turned out that this man Graham had owned a nightclub called Scruples on the Lytham seafront. The club was having a lot of trouble with a team of local lads and they had attacked Graham a few times.

Mick Papp, a local face who was supposedly related to Lazlo Papp, the three-time Olympic middleweight gold medal winner from Hungary, told the young manager, who was inexperienced in running nightclubs, that he knew a man that could sort this firm out and that he would bring him over the following weekend. I knew Mick Papp quite well from training at the Hills' boxing gym in Blackpool. When he came to see me he merely asked if I and any of my pals fancied a few weekends working in Lytham for a nice little earner. He never mentioned anything to me about the problems with the locals.

I travelled up with a big young lad named Dave Robertson, who had been doing some boxing training with me. Dave had never worked the doors before but said that he fancied giving it a go. We turned up at this club, Scruples, on the Saturday night at about nine o'clock. The police had closed the place down by ten-thirty.

The regular doormen were on duty. These were lads from Preston, about fifteen miles away. One of them was a big man a good few years older than me. We were stood to the side of the club chatting when a glass or a bottle smashed against the wall just above my head.

'What the fuck!'

Looking around the club I saw another glass winging its way towards us. Before it shattered against the wall I was moving towards the group of lads from where it had begun its journey. I had seen one lad's arm going downwards after completing the throw and so I was focused on him. I didn't know what was going on but I did know that he had just thrown at least one glass at me.

Bang! As soon as I reached him I belted him with a right hand. There was no point asking him why he had done it. He hit some fire doors behind him that led into a restaurant that was in the process of being renovated. The doors gave way and he fell into the other side. I followed him straight through the doors to administer further punishment but before I had got more than a of couple punches in, I was overwhelmed by a group of lads that came into the restaurant area after me.

It was touch and go for about thirty seconds until I realised that they were hitting or kicking each other as much as, if not more than, they were hitting me. The room was in the middle of a major refurbishment, so there were all sorts of tools and things lying around on the floor. The object that I decided on was a wooden ladder about six feet long. I picked it up by the rungs and started flailing about with it. I rammed the ends into their faces and balls and then I would swing it sideways, knocking their legs out from under them.

They had soon had enough of this. All of a sudden I was standing in the middle of the room holding this ladder and I was completely alone. I had taken a fair bit of punishment but I was still standing. Dropping the ladder, I went into the main room. The place was in a panic. I saw a group of about four lads kicking someone that was on the floor. All you could see of this person was these black shoes with white socks. I remembered taking the piss out of Dave when I picked him up: he was dressed in 'black and whites', as I had told him, but had these glaring white socks on.

I looked around to see where the rest of the door team had got to but they were nowhere in sight. I just flew straight into these lads, knocking the nearest two down with sheer body weight. The other two ran off, quickly followed by their two pals that I had knocked over. Wankers.

Helping Dave to get up, I was pleased to find that he was not badly hurt. They must have been getting in each other's way, as is usual when they attack a single person in numbers. The gang of local lads had all gone but there again so had the rest of the door staff, including Mick Papp. The police arrived and promptly closed the place. They were very interested in me and wanted to know who I was and where was I from.

When Mick Papp finally reappeared from wherever he had gone to, I got the full story from him. 'Why didn't you warn me, you daft cunt?' I asked him. At least we would have been expecting something.

The next weekend, Dave and I turned up at nine o'clock but this time we were prepared for a bit of action. Dave had decided that working the doors was not for him but there was no way that he would let me go there by myself. Top man Dave.

I had asked the manager for our wages from the previous weekend and the cheeky twat turned round and paid us both for one hour.

'It's not our fault the club was closed early,' he said.

I looked him straight in the eye.

'Whose fault was it then?'

'Yours,' he replied.

How the fuck I never hit him I don't know. The man's dead now so I won't speak ill of him, he obviously didn't know any better. Needless to say, we left them to it.

I managed to bump into quite a few of the faces that I could remember over the next few months and when I say bump, I mean bump. There were two brothers called Jones and another guy called Hedgehog, local hard cases with a load of idiots behind them who terrorised the town at that time. It seems the police put two and two together and got five, accusing me of an assault I wasn't involved in. Fortunately it came to nothing, but that's the way it goes.

Not long after, I was banged up in the cells again. A debt collection job had gone slightly wrong. I had turned up at the address, a house that had been converted into a number of flats, and rung the bell. Once I had found the correct flat I introduced myself to the gentleman that owed the debt. After he had screamed for a while, he ran down the stairs, out of the front door and was gone. His scream had not gone unnoticed and I was confronted by the landlord of the building. Seeing me in a suit and tie, the landlord jumped to the wrong conclusion and assumed I was a police officer.

'I knew he was up to no good,' he said to me, shaking his head. 'Would you like me to let you into his flat, officer?'

'That would be nice, if you don't mind.' I nodded and smiled sincerely at him.

Just then John Tate, who was driving the car I had come in, entered the building. I introduced him to the landlord as my colleague. I then explained to John that, as we were the police – wink, wink – the landlord was going to be kind enough to let us into the 'suspect's' flat. Tate was nearly weeing himself trying to keep his face straight.

Then to cap it all the landlord turned to face me as he was opening the flat door and pointed his finger at a wardrobe on the landing.

'He doesn't know that I know, but he sometimes hides things behind the wardrobe.'

The long and short of it was that John Tate and I end up getting arrested on a Friday night as we are turning up for work. I was actually nicked when I was in Steve Daley's car as a passenger. A police officer then jumped into the front passenger seat and made Steve drive to the police station. Steve was released when he was identified and they realised he had nothing to do with the case in question. When I spoke to him later, he told me, 'That was the scariest drive of my life. Every time I braked I was worried that something under my seat might slide forward and hit the copper's feet.' If that had happened we would have been looking at a lot of time. We ended up being charged with aggravated burglary. Fucking burglary, I ask you.

The police kept us both banged up over the weekend in the cells at Blackpool central police station on Bonny Street. On the Monday morning, John and I were brought up from the cells and put in front of the Blackpool magistrates. We were both refused bail and remanded in custody but only until the Wednesday, thankfully.

On the Wednesday morning, we were brought back into the same courtroom. I took a glance around the room to see who was present and was very surprised to find it was full of school kids, all aged around fourteen. Sharpie and a couple of other lads were hidden away in a corner trying not to be seen, to give us some moral support.

The detective in charge of the case was big, fat and horrible. When he was called up to present the police case, he turned in the witness box to point at me and said, 'This man and his associates are Blackpool's equivalent to the Krays' organised crime gang that terrorised London.' There was an audible gasp from all the spectators in the room, with all the school kids sitting up straight and taking a lot more interest in the case.

After about one hour of the prosecution slagging us, the defence solicitor managed to get a few words in. I had one spent conviction against my name and that was for the incident on the Isle of Wight when I was eighteen. Although John had some previous, he was clear at that time. The magistrates granted us bail. Some time later that day the individual who had made the accusations against us visited his own solicitor to help him get the police to let him withdraw the complaint. The police were not happy about this but in the end all charges against John Tate and myself were dropped.

I got into debt-collecting as a natural extension of door work. Doormen get approached with all kinds of propositions, especially for work that involves a bit of muscle. Sometimes you will be asked to collect a debt, and it's not uncommon to hear, 'He owes me this, if you go and get it you can have half.' It is hard to turn down the money and some doormen even become loansharks themselves. Debt collecting is all right so long as it doesn't become personal but when it does it can have dire consequences all round, as I would later learn.

10

Naughty

IT WAS A lovely Saturday early in the summer of 1988 or '89. My friend Mark Wood from Portsmouth had phoned to say he was up in Blackpool overnight, driving a minibus full of girls who were here on a hen night. I arranged to meet him early doors before I went to work at the Number Three pub on Whitegate Drive. The Number Three is a very nice locals' venue, rarely visited by holidaymakers. I phoned Sharpie, who had met Mark a few times, and asked him if he fancied a few drinks before he opened his club for the night, the Adam and Eve near Central Pier.

We met at the Number Three at about seven o'clock: Ian Sharples, Mark Wood, a lad called Peter Flackett and myself. We stood at the end of the long main bar in the big room having a quiet drink. The pub was quite busy with couples and generally nice people when all of a sudden a large team of lads entered, there must have been fifty of them. They were loud and boisterous from the moment they entered and within a few moments they were causing the regular customers to feel uncomfortable.

The licensee at that time was a man named Alan Ball (not the famous ex-Blackpool footballer). Alan did not have door staff on at the Number Three as usually there was no need. He knew that Ian and I were involved in nightclubs and security and came over to ask us if we could keep an eye on the situation while he phoned for the police. I remember saying, 'There's not a lot that we can do, but okay.'

Two minutes later, one of the group picked up a fire extinguisher and set it off. He sprayed a jet of water over the local customers in an arc that was heading towards us, causing people to jump up and run or even get under the tables. Now Sharpie and I were both suited and booted for work, in nice Boss suits and shiny shoes, you get the picture. Anyway this dick with the fire extinguisher sprayed the water across me at waist height and was moving on towards the lads. Now because I never flinched or moved but just stared at this dickhead, he came back to me and sprayed me up and down, laughing all the time.

I thought to myself, fuck you, you cunt; you are having it. I put my pint down on the bar and then just flew at him. He hit me on the chest with the extinguisher as I got to him but by then I was completely psyched up and did not feel a thing. I picked him up and bulled straight through his pals. I did not know it at the time but Ian had tried to grab my jacket to stop me, but having missed he came through right behind me, stopping any of this lad's pals from jumping on my back.

I actually carried this lad the full width of the pub, out of the main room and into a corner of the small annex bar. I slammed him down onto the floor and was just about to let him have a few right hands when a searing pain hit my left eye. Shaking my head to clear my vision, I saw I was spraying blood everywhere. I had been hit by a flying glass or bottle thrown by one of dickhead's pals. When I looked down at him he was actually smiling at me, the cunt.

On the floor next to his head lay a big crystal glass ashtray. Picking it up, I thought, this will wipe the smile of your face. It did. Glasses were still smashing on the wall behind me but no-one was grabbing me or throwing kicks or punches. I looked around. Sharpie was standing there with a stool in his hands, swinging like a dervish.

There was blood pouring from his mouth where a glass or bottle had caught him.

Dickhead was now unconscious, so I grabbed hold of a nearby stool and stood up. I noticed that my friend Mark, who is a black belt at karate, had come around from the side and was keeping some of them busy there. They had run out of glasses by now and looking at the nearest ones to us I could see the fear in their eyes. I have always been a strong believer in looking into the eyes, you can find the truth there.

I looked at Ian and said, 'Let's fucking do them.' We both went into them at the same time, swinging the small stools for all they were worth. Anyone who stayed in front of us copped a stool, a punch, an elbow or anything else we could hit them with. Believe me or not, we cleared them from the small bar area and then cleared them from the pub. When they were all outside some of them probably felt embarrassed and tried to rally the others to storm back in but every time they tried, we repulsed them. Eventually flashing blue lights announced the arrival of the boys in blue.

Nineteen men from Stoke-on-Trent were arrested at the scene. One of the lads from Stoke had brought a camera with him and had actually taken pictures of Ian and me laying into them with the stools. Sharpie and I both required hospital attention and so did about ten of them, including the daft twat who started it. Ambulances ferried the injured parties to the Victoria Hospital, where the police maintained a strong presence to stop any further fighting. Ian had about thirty stitches in a mouth wound and I had eight in a wound over my left eye. The doctors attending to my wound had finished before those stitching Sharpie, so I went to see him. The miserable twat only went and had me thrown out because I kept making him laugh and he said it hurt. Once we were fixed up we both went home and got changed, then we both went to work later that night. You can't keep a good man down.

Sixteen of the nineteen were released the next day but three were detained to appear in Blackpool Magistrates Court on Monday morning. I attended the court with my good friend John Tate. It turned out that one of the three lads from Stoke had a long list of previous convictions for violence and so he was remanded in custody. The other two were released on bail. We learned that the lads had been part of a three-coach-strong stag do from Stoke. Their coach had become separated from the others and they had stopped at the Number Three for a quick drink, hoping the other coaches would see them on their way into the town centre.

John and I debated what we would do if we had got nicked on a night out in another town before we had had a chance to spend any of our money. Taxi or train? If it was a taxi, they were gone; if it was the train, they were ours. We quickly made our way to the train station. We walked into the buffet bar at Blackpool North and there they were, not a care in the world, having a drink and a sandwich.

Sliding into the vacant seats next to them, I said, 'All right lads. Remember me?'

They both shook their heads and said, 'No.' Removing the sunglasses that covered a good part of my injury, I smiled and said, 'The last time you probably saw me you were throwing glasses at me.' Then I elbowed mine in the face and slammed his head into the wall whilst Tate did something similar to the man sat next to him. The buffet bar staff started screaming and shouting, saying that they were calling the police. I don't think they did in the end though because I never got a visit.

Mark Chester, the leader of Stoke's Naughty Forty hooligan firm, later wrote about this incident in his memoir *Naughty*. In his book Mark said there was about ten of us; there wasn't. Mark, who also wrote the sequel *Sex, Drugs and Football Thugs*, now lives in Blackpool and we have had a few laughs together about that night. He told me they still talk about it in Stoke.

Both Ian and I applied for criminal injuries, the compensation paid to victims of crime. We were both rejected and had to appeal. Before the appeal hearing, I was informed by a friend of mine in the Blackpool CID that it was the testimony of the investigating officer in charge of the case that if we had not been there, the incident would not have happened and that we were well-known as local villains. This was backed up by a copy of the original police report.

The day of the appeal, when it finally came around about two years later, was the same day that Ian Sharples, Graham Blow and I were going to Fuengirola in Spain for a two-week holiday and possibly a little bit of business. Luckily it was being held at a court venue in Manchester and it was early enough in the day so that I could attend it on the way to the airport. As I entered the appeal room in Manchester, I saw numerous solicitors and the copper in charge of the case, a detective sergeant from Blackpool, all sat around this big table.

'Well Mr Sinclair, why do you think that you deserve criminal injuries after you have already been refused?' asked the chairman of the appeal board.

I pulled out a copy of the police report and handed it to him, saying, 'If you read that sir, it makes me sound like a criminal, while I am in fact a happily married family man with one spent conviction from twelve to thirteen years ago. I am also a licensee and businessman.'

The detective sergeant in charge of the case was fuming and wanted to know where I had got a copy of his report. I smiled at him and said my solicitor had obtained it for me. I made another enemy that day but who cares, he should not have been such a dick. The appeal board apologised to me and awarded me £1,000. I went off to Spain on holiday in a very good mood.

When Ian's appeal came up, even though he was a

club owner he was not a licensee. They looked at his previous form and told him he was lucky he did not have to pay them. Oh well, win some, lose some. Life's hard, eh pal.

Things were going well in my personal life with Tanee so we took the next step and bought a house together on Elizabeth Street in Blackpool. The club was doing very well at that time and, due to a change in staff, Steven Swallow, who I had met for the first time on the night that I was stabbed, had joined the door team along with my good pal John Tate. The fourth doorman was a good Scottish lad named Glen Lawson – the lad I was talking to when Sharpie drove his car into me – and between us we had a very nice little team.

It was nearly closing time on a Saturday night and it had just gone bang off at the door with a team of lads trying to force their way in for a last drink. We ended up giving these lads a slap. One of them was knocked down onto the pavement and stayed down even when his pals backed off. We had to call for an ambulance and of course the police turned up without being invited. The bloke who had been injured was taken away to Victoria Hospital by the ambulance and Glen Lawson was taken into custody by the police for questioning.

By this time the club had closed and nearly every customer had left. I had seen some of the men that had been with the group involved in the trouble heading off up Dickson Road, opposite the club. Neither John Tate nor I had driven to work but Steve Swallow had, so I asked John to stay at the club and make sure Stan and Sheila, the owners, were okay with everything. Meanwhile Swallow drove us along Dickson Road looking for the men I had seen walking away. The road was quite busy, with club-goers heading out of the town centre. Driving slowly along, we saw three men walking north towards Gynn Square, eating kebabs.

'That's them,' said Swallow, nodding his head in their direction.

Looking up and down the road, I told Steve to drive on for about one hundred yards and park up. We got out of the car and took up a position that would enable us to intercept the three men. As they approached, we stepped into their path. I think I only got as far as saying, 'Right you cunts ...' but by then two of them had gone, they took off as if they had been fired from a rocket, one each side of me. The third one could not move by then; I had grabbed him by his throat and had him bent backwards over a waist-high wall. Swallow tried to catch the others but they were well in front of him so he gave it up as a bad job. I had got the information I had wanted by then, where they were from and the name of the lad in hospital.

Looking over the wall I saw it was about a twelve-foot drop onto a flat basement roof of a hotel. I glanced left and right to see if anyone was taking an interest but no-one seemed to be, so still having hold of the man's throat with my right hand I reached down and grabbed his crotch with my left and heaved him over the wall. Steve Swallow ran to the wall and looked over. The bloke was sprawled out on his back next to a skylight. Swallow looked over at me and said, 'Fucking hell Steve, you were lucky he never went through that skylight.'

I just shook my head and smiled at him. 'That's what I was fucking aiming for.'

I had learnt that the group had come from Fleetwood, a nearby town, and I also had the full name of the lad who was at the hospital. Getting into the car, we headed for Victoria Hospital. I wanted to have a quick chat with the injured party to make sure that no charges would be made against Glen.

When we entered the accident and emergency department, we looked around to make sure that there were no police present. I approached a nurse and in my politest manner said, 'Excuse me nurse, I am here about an incident that took place at the Just Ji's night club earlier. A man by the name of so-and-so was brought in by ambulance not too long ago.' The nurse must have looked at Steve Swallow and me and taken in that we were both over six feet tall and well dressed. Swallow had taken his bow tie off but he was still wearing his black suit and white shirt, while I was wearing a lounge suit and tie. The nurse must have just assumed we were police officers because she said, 'If you wait here, officer, I will get the staff nurse in charge.'

I looked at Steve Swallow and smiled. He grinned back at me.

'What the hell, let's run with it.'

The nurse in charge approached us carrying some paperwork. She had obviously been informed that we were two of Blackpool's finest because she just asked us what it was that we would like to know. We enquired after his condition and if it would be possible to interview him. It turned out that he had been admitted to a ward but he was not hurt too badly and no, he could not be interviewed until the morning. Thanking her for her help, we turned to leave and saw two CID officers enter through the main doors. As we walked past them they both nodded to us and said, 'Steve, Steve.' Once we got outside we both burst out laughing. How close! It turned out that the lads all played for the same amateur football team and were out celebrating a semi-final win, but five of them had to receive hospital treatment of some sort, including the guy who had gone over the hotel wall, who sustained a broken wrist. In the end no charges were brought against Glen.

It was announced that in November 1988, Sugar Ray Leonard was to fight the Canadian Donny Lalonde for the super middleweight and light-heavyweight world titles in Las Vegas. A few good friends and I decided we would like to go over to Vegas and watch the fight live. In the end there was Steve Swallow, Andy Harrison, Steve Warton and his girlfriend with their baby daughter Jamie, and me. When we arrived at Manchester Airport we met up with Dave 'Boy' Green and a bunch of his pals who were all going over to Las Vegas as well. I had met Dave some years before at the Foxhall pub on Blackpool's seafront when I had been one of the doormen there. One of my colleagues was refusing entry to a couple of men as I was walking past the door. My head nearly came loose doing a double-take: one of the men was Dave 'Boy' Green, the British boxer who had fought both Sugar Ray Leonard and Carlos Palomino for the world welterweight title. I quickly intervened and made sure that Dave and his pal both got a drink. Dave, who hails from East Anglia, already knew about someone doing an exhibition fight with Leonard on the *QE2* but he was surprised to find out it was me.

When we arrived in Las Vegas, Dave was invited to a private training session and photo shoot with the Leonard team. He invited me to go with him. Sugar Ray Leonard's face was a picture when we walked in. He was made up to see Dave Green and he was very surprised to see me there with him. I am pleased to say he did recognise me and I was also recognised by the press as the guy from the *QE2*.

Unbeknown to me, a documentary about Sugar Ray Leonard, Champion of Champions, had been repeatedly shown on American television in the lead up to the big fight and I was actually in it for about five minutes, along with Muhammad Ali, Marvin Hagler, Thomas Hearns, Roberto Duran, Dave Green and other greats of the ring. How about that for being in good company?

Steve Warton was stuck with Christine and baby Jamie, but for the rest of us it was party time. We hired a car and drove across the state line into Los Angeles for a couple of nights. That was an adventure by itself. Swallow and Andy started arguing about the driving and it ended up with them stopping the car in the middle of the freeway, getting out of the car and squaring up to each other. I had to jump into the driver's seat and get them back into the car before we were all killed. Once they had made up, and after we had travelled about one hundred miles, I jumped into the back to get my head down.

I was woken by the sound of them arguing again. I thought I would just lie there and ignore them both until I heard one of them say, 'Pull over and ask them guys.' Sticking my head up so I could see out of the window, I saw scruffy tenement buildings and a very rundown neighbourhood. Looking over to see what bunch of guys they were talking about, I saw we were just about to pull up to a large group of Hispanic homeboys. We were only cruising around lost in East LA. Seeing a new Ford Mustang hire car with three obviously lost white tourists pulling into the sidewalk, they must have thought it was Christmas come early and we were their presents.

'Don't stop here you daft twat, drive,' I shouted. 'Drive, drive.'

Seeing the men we were pulling over towards pulling guns and knives from their belts, Andy hit the accelerator just in time to get us out of there. Once we had calmed down, cleared the smell from the inside of the car and reached a safer location, we could see the funny side of it. It just goes to show, you may be streetwise in England but how naïve was that?

When we drove back into Las Vegas two days later, we passed a big sign that read

SHOOTING RANGE AT NEXT TURN OFF: MACHINE GUNS, AUTOMATIC WEAPONS FOR HIRE OR TO BUY.

What a sign that is to advertise your business. Neither Steve nor Andy had fired a gun before so we decided to see if it was open. When we entered the shop, it was outrageous: there was every type of gun that you could imagine, all for sale or hire. We ended up in the back with an Israeli Uzi nine-millimetre machine gun and a Mac10 machine gun plus a Magnum .44 revolver, a Smith and Wesson .38 revolver and a Beretta nine-millimetre semi-automatic handgun. I have never seen anyone's face change like Andy's the first time he held a hand gun with live ammunition in it. If I didn't know any better I would have sworn he was a psycho.

When we finally got to the fight, at the Caesar's Palace Hotel, we were all very excited. We had paid about £200 each for our tickets to the fight and so we were expecting good seats. But we ended up having to buy binoculars from the vendors, we were that far away. Still, the bouts were great and we had a good evening. We all had a great stay in Vegas and thanks to Dave 'Boy' Green we were introduced to a lot of ex and current world boxing champions and other celebrities like Bo Derek and Chuck Norris. Thanks Dave, top man.

Stan and Sheila decided to put Just Ji's up for sale, but at least they had the decency to keep the staff in the picture. Before it was sold, Steve Swallow had an offer to go to the Showboat and Waves, a new club on the promenade, as the head doorman, which we talked over and after some consideration he accepted. This turned out to be a top move for Steve, as the man he was working for, Stuart Kay, offered him extra contracts, enabling Steve to set up his own company, Swallow Security.

This left a gap in our team that was soon filled by another Steve (we like to keep it easy for people to remember names). Steve Daley was already working on the doors on Blackpool promenade with my friend Jimmy the Dancer. One night it had gone bang off with a gang of men from the north-east. One of these men grabbed hold of Steve Daley and was attempting to pull him out from the door and into the middle of his mates. All of a sudden the bloke's arm opened up to the bone. Someone had slashed out with a knife and had only just missed Steve's face. It was never proven who did it but Steve decided it was time to move away from the promenade. During the day he operated and ran his own gym that we all used regularly, called Sneakers. Steve is a big, strong, capable man who would be an asset to any door team in the country.

The new owners of the club were a couple named Bob and Jackie. They were lovely people who did not want to change a winning formula. The club continued to be very popular with the locals.

It was around this time that I met Peter McCarthy for the first time. Pete had moved to Blackpool from High Wycombe and was working for Stephen Hill's Northern Security as a doorman. Across the road from Just Ji's was a pub named the Station, where the door was manned by Northern Security men. Time and time again I witnessed trouble develop on the Station door and escalate into violence.

On this evening, I saw a large group of men arguing with the door staff at the Station. There was a sudden flurry of punches thrown between the two groups of men. I saw the doormen jump back inside the pub and slam the door closed. The only trouble was they had left one of their own men outside. I watched as this individual got knocked to the ground and then he was kicked as he was on the floor. He rolled under a car that was parked at the curb to try and get away from his attackers. All this time his colleagues stayed behind the locked doors of the pub, watching through the window. The group of men did not look like they intended to stop kicking the doorman at any time soon and his so-called mates didn't look like they were coming out to help him, so I thought to myself, fuck it, then I leapt the safety railing outside of Just Ji's, ran across the street and piled into them.

I dropped two of them before they knew I was there. By then I had bulled my way through them and put my back against the car and started banging with both hands. They had a little bit of a go for a couple of seconds but soon backed off when my lads came running from Just Ji's. When I had pulled the lad out from under the car and had made sure he was not too badly hurt, I looked him in the eye and told him to get some new mates. I then slated the other doormen who had finally emerged from their safe haven as cowards and wankers before returning to Ji's.

Luckily for me Bob and Jackie were both very understanding about us leaving their venue for that short period.

My best pal, Ian Sharples, had been arrested after a fight outside his club, the Adam and Eve on Chapel Street in Blackpool. Some lads from St Annes, a small town just south of Blackpool, had given Ian and his staff some shit and when Ian laid down the law they objected and offered up some violence in response. Ian obliged and ended up getting nicked for it. One lad ended up on a life support machine (I told you how easily it happens sometimes, other times you can jump all over them and they walk away unscathed). As luck would have it he made a full recovery. The police claimed that Ian had hit one or more of these lads with a battery.

'A car battery?' I asked.

'Don't be fucking clever Sinclair,' they replied.

Ian sometimes carried an Ever Ready battery in his pocket, it gave you something to play about with if you did not smoke when you were stood on a door and it also helped increase the power of a punch if held in a clenched fist.

We visited St Annes on numerous occasions, chasing the toerags all over the place. On one such occasion during Lytham Club Day there were four of us present when all of a sudden we were surrounded by about ten of the St Annes mob. They fronted us up, saying to Ian, 'We know who you are, but who are you?'

Andy Sharples replied first, 'I am Ian's brother.' Next was Ian Crawford, who introduced himself as Crowie, and then there was me.

'I'm Steve Sinclair.'

Thinking about it now, Ian had slapped three of them by himself at the Adam and Eve club, Andy was nearly as good as Ian, they would inevitably have heard of Crowie over the years as they grew up and they all knew my name. Some of them had probably been at the Scruples nightclub on the Lytham promenade a few years earlier when it had kicked off good style. They bottled it, but as the Jones brothers were not there and they were the ones that we were really hoping to have a quiet chat with, we couldn't do much about it at that time.

In the end Ian was sentenced to two years for this, eighteen months for that and nine months for something else. Luckily it was all to run concurrently, not consecutively, so it was two years in total instead of four years and three months. Crowie and I both attended Preston Crown Court for the verdict and I am not ashamed to say I shed a few tears when he was sent down. I had lost my best mate, for the time being.

11

Promises

IT WAS AROUND this time that tablets of the designer drug ecstasy were first introduced to the British public. It was portrayed as a 'love drug' in the national papers, where friends both male and female would start making out with each other when they'd taken one tablet. These pills might have sounded a bit suspect but before long everyone seemed to be using them. The clubs were soon full of people off their faces. There had always been drugs around – cannabis, amphetamine, LSD, cocaine – but these E's were classed as a designer drug and young clubbers all across the country wanted them.

Blackpool was, and still is, a major outlet for drug dealers. The number of nightclubs alone gives the dealers a massive customer base. There are lots of local drug dealers in the Blackpool area that would probably have no trouble keeping the clubbers supplied but there have always been a large number of Liverpool or Manchester firms too who have tried to take control of the market.

The first time I ever tried ecstasy was on a lads' night out, when one of my mates turned up with some. These were the classic doves that were selling then for about £15 each tablet. About twenty minutes after I had dropped my first E, I turned into superman, I didn't think that I could fly or anything like that, I just felt WOW. I ended up picking up Steve Warton and Mick Creasy, who are both big blokes, one under each arm and running around the club.

There was a huge demand for ecstasy all over the country and Blackpool was no different. Certain people jumped on the bandwagon and started importing the drug into the town. I didn't mind using the stuff but there was no way that I was going into the business of supplying it; I would not want my family to suffer the disgrace of me being known as a drug dealer. I would rather get sent down for doing someone, even if it was a copper. However, my friends and I would often be asked to provide protection or enforcement for some of these dealers. The trouble here was that we were good friends with some of these individuals and our association was sometimes taken the wrong way by police forces, especially the Blackpool force. Bouncers or door staff across the country were starting to become main players in the drug trade, be it in supply or enforcement. The job was changing.

A big part of door security in Blackpool has always been looking after any celebrities that are appearing in shows in the town. This went back to the days of Samantha Fox, the hugely popular Page Three girl, and TV actors like Lewis Collins from *The Professionals*, right up to today's celebrities like Jordan. One evening I was stood by the door at Just Ji's when my pal Ian came through the door with a very well-known snooker player in tow. After saying hello to Sheila, the owner, who always did the cash desk herself, Ian asked if he could have a quick word.

Moving downstairs he introduced the snooker player to me, then in the same breath said, 'Steve, can you take this, I think we are being followed by the Old Bill?' He then passed me something that I put in my pocket.

'Yeah, no problems mate,' I replied as they wandered off into the club.

I thought I would check out what he had passed me.

It was only a big bag of charlie. Result!

After an hour or so had passed, Ian came back over to see me and said, 'I think we are okay, there doesn't seem to be anyone following us now, can I have it back please pal.' He held out his hand.

'Oops, sorry Ian, I thought you had given it to me,' I replied, handing back the nearly empty bag. It was worth it to see the look on the snooker player's face, he was nearly in tears.

Drugs or alcohol have the effect on people that they think they are invincible or at least a lot more capable than they really are. The new trend of clubbers taking ecstasy gave doormen all over the country problems. We consistently had to visit the local council estates of Grange Park, Mereside and even Fleetwood, where lads who had been under the influence of drugs had caused problems for us at our club. Sometimes we would go to their houses and put their front doors through but if they lived with their families we would end up going to the local pubs, where things could soon get very lively. We managed well enough to get our message across: Fuck with us at our place of work and we will find you.

June 12, 1989, Sugar Ray Leonard versus Thomas Hearns II, in Las Vegas again. How could I get to this one? Tanee and I had been talking about getting married. The trouble now was, I knew she was not keen on flying. But it had to be worth a try.

Yes! She was up for it; I knew there had to be a reason for me wanting to marry her.

Everything was arranged and the tickets were booked when Tanee asked me, 'Aren't you going to have a stag night before we go away?' What a girl.

It was all arranged for a big do but lads started to drop out one by one when their girlfriends or wives found out where we were going. In the end Steve Swallow, Glen Lawson and I finished work at Just Ji's on the Sunday morning and then drove all the way to Harwich and caught the cross-Channel ferry to Holland for a few days in Amsterdam.

We had heard all sorts of stories about how you get approached in the street by black men trying to sell you all sorts of drugs. We had checked up on what types of things were legal and what weren't. In Amsterdam you can go into a bar or a café and ask for a menu that shows you what drugs they sell on the premises. When we arrived in the city centre we picked a little hotel near to the train station. Within five minutes of us booking in, the place was surrounded by armed police officers.

We all looked at each other as if to say, 'What have you done now?'

Fortunately they were not there for any of us. They actually arrested someone who was in the bar beneath the hotel. When they brought him outside, he was handcuffed with his hands behind his back. All of a sudden he headbutted one of the coppers right in the face and dropped him. Fuck me, what a party town this is, I thought. The remaining police officers laid into this bloke with batons and boots until he was a mess.

Right there and then we decided to be on our best behaviour for the next few days.

The first night when we went out and about, we kept waiting for the dealers to 'pssst' us to let us know they were selling. Nothing, not once, not a black man, Arab or anyone else. Every time we walked nearby they would all put their heads down and blank us. I don't know if we looked like undercover police; but in the end I was *pssst*ing them like mad. We got sorted in the end.

Tanee and I flew out to Los Angeles early in June of 1989. She had to take herbal valiums to calm her down, bless her. After a few days in LA we drove to San Francisco to stay with friends who had moved there from Blackpool, Jane and Mark Singleton. Jane had been friends with Tanee for years and before she married Mark she had dated my pal Robin Thompson for a time.

After a few days with Mark and Jane we drove through to Vegas in time for the big fight. The atmosphere at Caesar's Palace was amazing. This was a fight long-awaited: Leonard and Hearns were both all-time greats and though Sugar Ray had won their first, classic encounter years earlier, this was a genuine even-money contest. The build-up had been very impressive and the evening was a sellout.

The Leonard camp had given me a white Franklin Boxing tracksuit with Sugar Ray Leonard emblazoned across the back so I decided to wear it that evening to the fight. I had bought good tickets because the last time I was there with the lads we were so far back we'd had to buy binoculars from a drinks vendor. Tanee and I were escorted to our seats, only to find they were only smack bang in the middle of about one hundred black Thomas Hearns fans. I don't know who looked more shocked, us or them, I must have looked like a snowflake in a coal cellar and don't forget what I was wearing. Luckily they turned out to have a good sense of humour and when they found out we were English they gave me back all my jewellery and money. Only joking.

The big guy who was sat next to me looked very familiar. He turned out to be the actor Danny Glover, who was famous for his role opposite Mel Gibson in the *Lethal Weapon* films.

The fight was another thriller and was declared a draw, which to be truthful was a bit of a result for Leonard.

Tanee and I were married at the Chapel of the Bells on The Strip in Las Vegas two days after the Leonard-Hearns fight, on June 14. We had a big stretch limo and a post-wedding dinner at Caesar's Palace with our friends from Blackpool who now live in the States. It was a great day for both of us, although we did get some sad news later that day. Treeve, one of Tanee's two younger brothers, had died as a result of injuries that he had received in a garden shed fire in Oldham.

Not long after we had returned from America, I was approached one evening by an area manager for a private pub company who asked if I would manage a Blackpool town centre bar named Promises for the owner, a man who lived on Jersey, in the Channel Islands. I was upfront with the man who approached me and explained to him that I might not be able to get a Justices' Licence if the police objected. He thought about it for a while and then told me that if I was interested he would look into it for me.

I replied that I was very interested.

About a month later, I was in front of Brian Reeves, the clerk to the court for the Blackpool magistrates, applying for a full-on Justices' Licence to run Promises nightclub on Corporation Street, in a key location right in the centre of town. To the dismay of the Blackpool police, the magistrates granted me a protection order for the licence.

My new bride was not very happy about us having to move into the pub/club but it was part of my contract that I lived on the premises. I had visited the club on a few different occasions since being approached. At that time it was being run by two gay men and although it was still quite busy it was just beginning to lose its popularity with the local crowd. The door was being run by a group of Scottish lads, Gilby Joe Martin, Neil and a couple of others, who decided to move on when they heard that it was me that would be taking over. It was only when I compared the door takings on my first weekend with what had previously been declared that I realised why. All the male staff resigned and all the females remained. I was very grateful for this and still count Linda and Shirley as close friends.

Tanee had worked for the same company in Blackpool since she was about twenty-five years old and although she did not mind helping me run the place, she was not willing to leave her job. I still needed some more reliable staff and at short notice. Jimmy the Dancer, my pal from Lips, was available to work so I offered him a job as my assistant. He could live in, as there were plenty of spare rooms, be the DJ in the club and look after the cellar.

Promises at that time was only open in the evening. There were no exterior windows, as these had been covered over because of the late licence and other licensing requirements at that time. The club was on street level on the corner of Corporation Street and Birley Street, with the main entrance being on Corporation Street and the fire exit and cellar doors being on Birley Street.

The club revived and became a very busy locals' venue. I decided to hire my door staff from Stephen Hill of Northern Security rather than put lads on myself, on the proviso that I could choose them myself. This was mainly to keep the police off my back, as they were still not too happy with me getting my licence. I chose two lads, one named Steve (Scouse) and the other John. They might not have been the best doormen in the world but what a laugh. It was like having Laurel and Hardy on the door. Every two minutes one of them would say to the other, 'That's another mess you've got me into.'

One Saturday afternoon, before the all-day licensing came into force, I had taken a booking for a private stag do behind locked doors. The party of men from Bradford came to Blackpool earlier on that day and had spent some time with me in Promises and then gone to the Pleasure Beach for a couple of hours, before returning to Promises prior to me closing the doors at three o'clock in the afternoon. The lads were all in fine fettle as they say and were enjoying the strippers when two brothers decided to start fighting. With there being no-one else on the premises except for the staff, the stag party and the strippers, I was quite willing to let them fight as long as it did not escalate with other members of their party joining in.

But no, Laurel and Hardy pushed them through the side door onto Abingdon Street just as a special constable was walking past. Within minutes the street was blocked off by police riot vans, with another four or five vehicles full of uniforms screeching to a halt with full sirens wailing. Talk about overkill. The only person actually detained was one of the two brothers.

A few days later, I received a summons. The police had dug up an old law stating that drunks should not be on licensed premises. It actually appeared in some of the daily papers saying that no-one had been prosecuted under this law in England for over one hundred years. When I attended court I found the case was being held in the juvenile court (just goes to show, eh!). The police put approximately twelve witnesses on, all of them police officers, ranging in rank from the special constable that started it all to the chief inspector in charge of the shift. Every one of those coppers swore blind that the detained man was drunk or that he smelled of alcohol or was glassy eyed.

When they finally got me into the witness box, I was asked, 'Did you think that the man was drunk?'

I replied, 'No sir, I did not.'

'Well Mr Sinclair, how do you explain the detainee's breath smelling of alcohol?'

'He had just been drinking beer but it does not make him drunk, sir.'

'What about his eyes being glazed then?'

'He may have been on medication or drugs, sir.'

This went on for a short while and in the end I was found not guilty. This was because at that time there was no sobriety test and they could not breathalyse or blood test him as he was not driving a vehicle.

A week or so later, the club was open. It was a Friday or Saturday night, about ten o'clock. Scouse or John called me over to the front door. Crossing the road outside the club was Superintendent McKay, head of the Blackpool police, accompanied by a couple of other officers. Now McKay was a born-again Christian type who carried a swagger stick under his arm. He had little or no tolerance for me, as he suspected I was a criminal.

On entering the club he looked at me and said, 'Ah, Mr Sinclair, I believe you have a drug problem in here.'

The pompous twat. I looked him straight in the eye and shook my head, saying, 'No we don't, we can get anything you want.'

Scouse and John's mouths were both hanging open, they could not believe I had just said that to him. To tell the truth I hadn't meant to, it's just that I found him so arrogant that it just came out. He very nearly went epileptic. He started shaking and his face turned beetroot red. Turning on his heels, he walked out without saying another word.

I knew that the police would not take this lying down, but when I was pulled in for questioning over the death of a young Scotsman who had died from taking an ecstasy tablet, I thought this was taking things too far. Apparently the young man, only about nineteen years old, bless him, had been in Promises on the evening he died and the police were alleging he had got the tablet there. After being questioned at the police station, I was informed that I would have to attend the inquest that would be held by the Blackpool Coroner and, depending on the verdict, I might still face charges.

Obviously the weeks leading up to the inquest were not a very happy time. There had been quite a few articles in the papers about young people dying from taking ecstasy tablets and it was being taken seriously by the authorities. When the day finally came around, I decided to attend the inquest by myself rather than turning up with a few associates. I felt more like a criminal there than I ever have in a Crown Court. After answering some questions,

I sat watching the young man's family, who had travelled down from Scotland. The way they kept looking at me made me feel terrible. I wanted to shout to them, 'It's fuck all to do with me.'

Finally the pathologist took the stand. During the evidence he presented, it was proven that the ecstasy tablet that had killed the young lad had been in his bloodstream before he arrived in Blackpool, let alone Promises. Once the pathologist had finished giving his report, Sammy Lee, the Coroner, asked me to stand up and apologised to me. He told me I was free to leave. I heard no apologies from the police but what the hell, fuck them.

As I was leaving the court, I gave my condolences to the family of the deceased. It turns out that a person can be allergic to ecstasy and just one tablet can kill them, whereas someone else can take loads in one session with seemingly no ill effects.

12

A Helping Fist

IN A POWDER-KEG town like Blackpool, where people
come to let their hair down, lose their inhibitions and
drink themselves insensible, it is very easy to find yourself
embroiled in incidents that elsewhere would seem abnormal.
The bizarre is a daily occurrence in working-class British
seaside resorts, and behaviour that would be unacceptable
anywhere else somehow becomes the norm. You never know
when you wake up in the morning (or afternoon if you have
had a late night) what the day is going to bring.

Tanee had returned to the flat above Promises after
taking her Yorkshire terriers for a walk. She was crying
her eyes out in anguish and carrying one of the dogs in her
arms. I immediately thought that one of them must have
been run over or knocked down by a car. At the time I was
not overly impressed with her dogs. They would not get
on with my bull mastiff, Thumper, and I had to keep him
separated from them, which was not that easy in a flat.

It turned out that whilst my wife was walking down the
street with the three yorkies – Sammy, the father, Mitsie,
the mother, and Clyde, the son – a group of men walked
towards her. She moved to the side of the pavement to give
them plenty of room but one of them, being a dickhead,
decided to kick one of them like you would a rugby ball.

Now by the time Tanee had got the dogs indoors and
upstairs into the flat, Sammy was starting to recover. My

wife had believed him to be dead so she was obviously upset. When she explained the full story to me, I was fuming. I cannot stand people that hurt animals. I am a strong believer in what they do to the animal should be done to them.

Getting as much of a description of the men as my wife could remember, I went looking for them. As I was leaving the building, Jimmy the Dancer was returning from wherever he had been at the time. He could tell by my face that something had happened and once I had explained the situation, he volunteered to come with me. Good lad.

We looked in every pub in the immediate vicinity and finally found them in the ground floor bar of the Clifton Hotel, on the corner of the promenade and Talbot Square. About twelve of them stood around the bar area waiting to be served. Two or three fitted the descriptions that my wife had given. I have to admit that my arse was twitching a bit right then, given their numbers, but when I thought about what that cunt had done to Sammy I stepped forward. I raised my voice so they could all hear me.

'Excuse me lads, which one of you fucking heroes likes to kick dogs?'

Everything went quiet, but a few of them stole quick glances at one lad that fit Tanee's description.

'Well, was it you, you prick?' I asked, focusing on the lad that the others had looked over at.

Obviously he denied it and by then the group had seen that there were only the two of us, so they started to feel a bit braver. I would not just walk away, so I said, 'Seeing as you have only just bought your drinks, it will give me time to go and get my wife, who will definitely be able to point out to me the one responsible, okay? And when she does, I am going to kick him up the fucking promenade.' With that I turned around and walked out.

Jimmy looked at me with what could only be described

as relief on his face. 'Thank fuck for that,' he said. 'I thought you were just going to lay into them.'

I smiled at him and replied, 'I'm daft at times but I'm not that daft.'

'What are you going to do now?' he asked nervously. 'Are you going to get Tanee?'

'Don't be daft. I am going to phone Ian, Frank and Joe.'

Once I had explained the story to them, all three were at the club within ten minutes. Jimmy was relieved to be let off the hook, as he had jobs to do before the club opened, but he had been there for me if needed. When we entered the corner bar of the Clifton Hotel it was empty. Big surprise. I asked the bartender if he had heard where the lads who were in ten minutes ago were going next.

'Yates's Wine Lodge.'

Yates's is in Talbot Square, just across the road from the Clifton Hotel. Pausing at the door of Yates's, I could see inside. It was quite busy but there at the end of the bar were the lads we were looking for. The head doorman at Yates's was Tommy Baldwin. I knew Tommy from the old days at George Hill's boxing club. When I had explained the situation, Tommy told the rest of the security team what was about to happen and that they should stay out of it. He also said to them, 'It won't last long anyway.' Bless him.

In Tommy's own words:

> I watched Sinclair walk over to this team of lads at the end of the bar. Sharples, Tonner and Joe Sweeney walked behind him. He placed his arms around the shoulders of the nearest two men that had their backs to him and said something to them. Then he smashed their heads together and stepped through into the rest of the group, followed by his pals. It was all over in seconds. They literally demolished the group. Sinclair then walked over to one of the men that was on the floor, said something to him and then kicked him in the head. Then all four turned and walked out, only

stopping at the door to apologise and also to say thank you to us for not getting involved.

The phone was ringing non-stop right next to my head. I opened my eyes and looked at the clock next to the phone; it was half past six in the morning. I had only come to bed two hours before after a heavy session downstairs in the club. I picked up the phone and growled into it, 'Hello.'

'Hello, is that Mr Stephen Sinclair, the landlord of Promises?' asked the voice on the other end.

'Yes it is,' I grunted.

'Hello Mr Sinclair, this is WPC so-and-so from Black-pool police station. One of our officers is at your door but he cannot get your attention.'

'Okay, tell him I will be with him in a minute,' I said, falling out of the bed. I looked over at Tanee but she was still fast asleep. It's funny, she could sleep through an earthquake but if I try sneaking in late she always wakes up. Pulling my dressing gown on, I walked down the three flights of stairs to the ground floor.

The family and staff always used the side entrance to Promises on Birley Street, so that is where I automatically went. I opened the door and stepped out. There was no one there. Being in my dressing gown, I stepped back inside and closed the door. I then walked through the club to the front door and started unlocking it, shouting, 'With you in a second.' Once I had unlocked and unbolted the oversize front door, I pulled it open.

My first thought was, *fuck me, it's obviously not a parking ticket.*

'Get your hands in the air, step outside and kneel down on the ground.'

Police cars were blocking the street outside the club and there was a number of armed policemen pointing big fuck-off guns at me. A senior officer shouted at me through a loudspeaker, 'Show me your hands, lie down, look at me ...' and all that bollocks. Then I heard, 'Stephen Sinclair, we are arresting you on suspicion of armed robbery. We have warrants to search these premises and your home address.' I smiled and thought to myself, Tanee won't sleep through this.

I was dragged off to Blackpool Central police station in handcuffs. Here we go again. Once I had been processed, they escorted me to a cell. On the way, I saw them bringing in Frank Tonner, also in handcuffs.

'What have you been up to Frank?' I asked him with a smile.

'No talking, get them away from each other,' screamed one of the cops.

In the end there was about six of us banged up, all waiting to be questioned about an armed bank robbery. A bit of advice for you if you have never been arrested: always ask for a brief, or solicitor, as soon as you are being processed by the custody sergeant. They cannot question you until he or she arrives. This enables you to either get a few hours rest or it gives you time to get your head together and think about what you are going to say. It is a fact that most crimes are solved by confessions without solicitors present or when some bastard has grassed you up.

There had recently been an armed robbery at the Midland Bank in Oxford Square, Blackpool, and the police in their wisdom had come to the conclusion me and some of my friends, or 'known associates', were responsible for it. Masked gunmen wearing army-type camouflage jackets had stolen a large amount of cash from the bank during an armoured van delivery.

When my interview began, the officer in charge produced a black balaclava helmet, a camouflage jacket, some shotgun cartridges and a few Midland Bank bags. *Oops!* Thank God my alibi was airtight. I had to explain that

I went clay pigeon shooting quite regularly, and that I had received the bank bags from the Post Office when I acquired change for the pub. We were kept in the cells overnight and released the following morning on part four bail. No formal charges were ever brought against me or anyone else pulled in that day. I could not believe that the Blackpool police would think I would do something like that on my own doorstep.

It was a midweek lunchtime and I was stood at the bar in Promises talking to some customers when Tanee walked through the door. I was surprised to see her because she works during the day as the company secretary of Stardream and Party House, a company that specialises in audio and lighting equipment, amongst other things, for the leisure industry.

'Hello, what are you doing here?' I asked.

'I have just been to the doctors, can we go upstairs,' she replied.

Once we were upstairs she sat me down and told me that she was pregnant. Tanee at that time was thirty-four years old and I was thirty-two. Kelly my daughter from my first marriage was twelve years old now, but what the hell, I was over the moon. The baby was due some time in December, what a top Christmas present that would be for the two of us.

Blackpool has always been very popular with visiting football fans whose team has been playing either at Bloomfield Road or at nearby towns like Preston, Blackburn, Bolton or Burnley – and sometimes even as far away as Manchester. Football firms of the stature of Chelsea, Leeds and Birmingham City would come to Blackpool and cause murders, fighting with each other or groups of holidaymakers and bouncers. Pubs like the Dutton Arms on South Promenade or the Manchester or Foxhall would be targeted and wrecked, depending on the strength of the door teams. When I had worked at the Foxhall we would have bats and sawn-off pool cues ready at hand to fend off these gangs and sometimes the fighting would reach as far as the Manchester pub, which is about four hundred yards away. If there are too many of them, you have to protect the tills and bar staff until the police arrive. Even then they might not come inside, the soft cunts. Many a time I have seen the police wait for the fighting to calm down before they will enter a venue.

In those days, opposing firms might meet up by accident and end up fighting in your club or on the streets of Blackpool, but nowadays it is more like a military exercise. Opposing firms can arrange meetings online or by using mobile phones, they can check on the internet for the names and addresses of any pub or club in any town and they can find out how to get to them just as easily. They can even print a map off from the auto route site of the surrounding streets.

One Saturday night at about eleven o clock, Ian Sharples, who had recently been released from jail, and I had gone for a walkabout around the town and ended up in a club on Topping Street that was now called Le Cage. This was the club that used to be known as Secrets. While we were there, one of the lads who worked behind the bar for me at Promises, by the name of Carl, finally found me. He was a bit stressed at the time because he had been running around looking for me.

'Steve, it has gone bang off at the club, there are a load of football fans in from Macclesfield.'

I didn't even know Macclesfield had a football team.

As we were making our way towards Promises we were met by Pete McCarthy, the 'ginger-headed one' **(see XX)**, who told us that these boys had let off some CS gas and

Steve Sinclair, pictured when working for Swallow Security for a feature that appeared in the *Guardian* newspaper. He is now training and development manager for Northern Security.

Pompey boot boys on the town in Blackpool, Easter 1976. From left: me, Dave Hayward, Pete Juggins and Nick Scutt. This was in the Foxhall pub, where I would later work as a doorman.

My old Portsmouth mate, karate expert Mark Wood, my sidekick in many a misadventure.

Captain of the Royal Engineers army boxing team, 1980. I was regimental light-heavyweight champion. Our sparring sessions with the Paras were legendary.

Part of the *QE2* rugby team about to play a game in Japan in the shadow of a smoking Mount Fuji. I'm furthest on the right.

Working the door of the Foxhall on Blackpool's central promenade, in my velvet bow tie and jacket. Class! From left: Robin Thompson, unknown, Gary and Deirdre Wade and me.

Boxing an exhibition against the great Sugar Ray Leonard on board the *QE2*. People often ask me who won, a Blackpool bouncer or one of the greatest boxers ever? Who do you think!

The heavy mob. From left: drug dealer Mark 'Magoo' McGovern, heavyweight boxer and security boss Dave Garside, unknown, Steve Warton, Ian Sharples, Steve Daley and me.

Some of the firm. From left: Joe Sweeney, Frank Tonner (inserting a chicken drumstick into his ear), me and the unmistakeable Jimmy the Dancer.

Stuart 'Iron Balls' Jackson (left), Barbara (godmother to my daughter Christie) and Glen Lawson at the Cotton Club.

Ginger-headed firebrand Pete McCarthy at his wedding to Susan, the former wife of Princess Diana's bodyguard, Trevor Rees-Jones

The side of Blackpool the tourist brochures like to project: tram rides, amusements and the Tower. But the town has a dark side too.

The boys are back in town. Facing the camera from left are Steve Swallow, myself, Ian Sharples and Andy Harrison in Promises, the town centre pub/club I took over.

Ladies' night with a difference: that's me, Sharon and Jimmy the Dancer helping out at an Ann Summers party at Promises. The organisers insisted on female staff only but we compromised and 'dragged up' instead.

John Tate, a great character, now sadly no longer with us. John accompanied me on many a revenge mission.

Steve (left), better known simply as 'Scouse', and John, my doormen at Promises nightclub. It was like having Laurel and Hardy on the door and there was never a dull moment.

With former champ Dave 'Boy' Green (centre) on the way to watch
Sugar Ray Leonard fight the Canadian Donny Lalonde in Las Vegas.
Steve Swallow is to the left of Green and Andy Harrison to the right.

Reunited with Ray Leonard in Vegas. I'd been
wondering what had happened to him since
our previous encounter! The boy done good.

Tanee and I are married in the Chapel of the Bells on The Strip in Las Vegas in June 1989. We also took in the second Ray Leonard-Tommy Hearns fight on our trip.

Likely lads Paul Jonas and Billy Ferris in the Verona Hotel. Billy is currently serving life for murder. I got to know him well after he dated my sister Lorraine.

Paul Ferris, the infamous Glasgow godfather and brother to Billy.

With Charlie Kray and Sharpie. We got to know many London faces over the years and did so much 'business' down there that we became known as the Park Lane Boys.

The old school at a sportsman's evening at Old Trafford in Manchester. The front row, from left, is Paul Kirby, me, big Stuart and Dinger.

Left to right: Big Stu, Alan Wilson, Glen Walsh and Glen's dad, Michael 'Mixie' Walsh, on a trip to Cuba. Mixie is a Blackpool legend who has known every major villain from the Kray twins onwards.

A proud day: graduating with a Professional Certificate in Education in 2005. I became the first person in my immediate family to earn any kind of degree.

BLACKPOOL AND
THE FYLDE COLLEGE
An Associate College of Lancaster University

With my girls at my fiftieth birthday party in Blackpool in 2007. Left to right: Christie, my youngest, Kelly, and Tanee, my wife.

that the police and fire brigade were at the club. We turned onto Birley Street, which runs along the side of the club. Birley Street is only about one hundred yards long and at the bottom, where it meets Corporation Street, we saw flashing blue lights. The police were holding back some locals and my security staff while a group of lads were walking up the street towards us. There was probably about fifteen of them and they were turning back to face the club and jeering at the police and locals.

'This is them,' said Pete, looking across at me.

The police were obviously shorthanded as they had not got involved with any arrests. At that time CS gas was not classed under the firearms legislation, as it is now. The Macclesfield crew were oblivious to us walking towards them, they were more interested in taking the piss out of those outside the club.

Sharpie saw me taking off my watch and did likewise. Looking at the group of idiots coming towards us, I noticed that some of them were carrying bottles or glasses they had taken from my club. I said to young Carl, the barman, 'Don't you get too involved. As we hit them, you go straight through them and get down the street and to the club.'

The nearest one to me raised both his arms as if to chant the name of their football club, but he never got that far. I sparked him with a big right hand and moved into the others. Sharpie, Pete and the young barman all flew into them at the same time.

A lot of them broke and ran straight past us but some of them recovered faster than the others and tried hitting us with, or throwing, the bottles or glasses they were carrying. Once they had thrown them, they too legged it to join their pals.

A loud cheer went up from outside the pub once they realised what had happened and who we were. The police officers present outside Promises had their work cut out trying to hold back the crowd; but as soon as we got back inside the pub everything quietened down.

We had many big fights at Promises, but as far as I can remember this was the only time that any firm emptied the place. And of all places, it was Macclesfield!

13

The Park Lane Boys

IAN SHARPLES HAD been released from jail after eighteen months for the fight at the Adam and Eve club. Without Ian there the club had gone to pot, as Ian's partner was not as on-the-ball as Ian was. So now he had to find something else to do. The dance scene was underway big-style in the cities but there was nowhere in Blackpool catering to that market at the time. He decided it was about time someone did cater for it.

The old Bierkeller opposite the Butlins Metropole hotel and above Bunters nightclub had been vacant for some time, so Ian went to have a look at it. The premises proved to be suitable and so Ian leased it there and then, though he had to employ a licensee to front it for him. Where he came up with the name Shaboo from I have no idea – unless it was the drugs. Anyway, it turned out to be a major success. Ian brought in a DJ from Manchester called Sasha. Although he wasn't very old he was a very well known DJ and already earning £1,000 a night. The police finally got the place shut down through overcrowding, which cost Ian a few pounds in fines.

One of those who started to frequent the Shaboo club and had introduced himself to Ian was a man called Paul Jonas. Paul was from the Walthamstow area of London. He was short and fat but larger than life, a proper Cockney wideboy with a heart of gold. He was also associated with Charlie Kray and a number of other villains from all over the country. He and his family moved up to Blackpool after buying into the hotel business. It was quite funny because Paul had a hotel, his mum had one and his dad had one, and they were all on the same road. Paul owned the Verona Hotel on Tyldesley Road.

Ian was over at my place early on a Saturday evening before his club opened its doors when someone came in and asked him if he would get in touch with Paul Jonas at the Verona. Ian used the pub phone to contact Paul. It turned out that he had a large group in from Yorkshire and he needed to 'have a word' with a couple of the men. Would it be possible for Ian to get some back-up over to the hotel as soon as possible? Ian explained the situation to me and asked me if I would go with him, saying that this Paul was a nice bloke and that I would get on well with him. We went to the hotel and sorted out the problem easily enough.

Paul was very grateful and asked us to stay for a drink. Once we were settled in the hotel's private bar, Paul pulled out a large bag of charlie and offered it around. This might not sound out of sorts, but he offered it with a teaspoon.

'No worries lads,' he said, putting one up each nostril.

I met many infamous people through Paul. One of the funniest incidents was when he again rang through about a problem. It was a summer afternoon in the middle of the season. Something had happened between Paul and the owners of another hotel around the corner from the Verona. Ian and I turned up at the Verona to find Paul in a bit of a state. He had had a row with the two guys that owned this other hotel and apparently they had threatened to either do something to Paul himself or to smash his hotel windows. He kept on going on about how big these two guys are and how he could not do anything by himself. We told him not to worry and that we would go and have a chat with these two geezers.

Just as we were walking out of the door Paul said, 'Oh, by the way, these two blokes are both gay and the hotel is for gays.'

'Oh, by the fucking way!' I said, looking at him with disgust. 'We were just going to go around to this hotel and have a bit of a chat with two big blokes who now turn out to be two gays? You cunt.'

I turned around to say something to Ian but he had disappeared back into the Verona. A minute later he came back out of the hotel wearing one pink Marigold rubber glove.

I looked at him with what must have seemed a bewildered expression, because he just said, 'I'm not getting HIV or Aids if I have to punch some queers.' With that he set off walking down a busy street towards this gay hotel wearing one pink rubber Marigold washing-up glove. I love that guy.

Needless to say, they would not let us into the hotel. They threatened to phone the police, panicking, but I'll tell you something: they could not take their eyes off Ian's pink rubber glove. God knows what they thought that was all about.

Some weeks later, Paul Jonas walks into Promises with two men and introduces them to me.

'Steve, this is my good friend Charlie and his son Gary.'

I shook hands with both of the men, saying to the older one that he seemed familiar and had I met him before?

'No,' he replied, 'you have probably seen me on the television or in the papers.'

'Oh yeah?' I said to him. 'What are you in and which character do you play?'

What a fucking knob I am. It turns out that it was only Charlie Kray, older brother to the notorious London crime twins Ronnie and Reggie. Still, we had a good laugh about it then and for some time after.

Charlie might have been a proper villain to some people but he was a top gentleman whom I was proud to know. He and his good lady at that time came to Blackpool quite often and when my daughter Christie was christened he bought us a lovely quilt and gave us a card with a £50 note in it for her.

Over the next few months we also met up with Eric Mason, a well-known London villain from the Kray firm and author of *The Brutal Truth*. This was through Michael Walsh, better known as 'Mixie', a living legend in certain circles. I believe that Eric Mason is currently ghostwriting a book on the exploits of Mixie Walsh.

Now at this time we had a nice little firm operating. There was Ian Sharples, Frank Tonner, Joseph Sweeney and yours truly. I first met Frank at Just Ji's nightclub when Steve Swallow wanted a night off. He brought in this young, fresh-faced kid and introduced him to me. He looked about twelve at the time but Swallow vouched for him.

Looking Frank up and down, I noticed that he was wearing a pair of Kickers. Now that wasn't too bad but they still had the leather tag on them. Without saying anything, I went to the office and borrowed a pair of scissors. When I got back to where the lads were standing, I squatted down and cut off the tag, then passed it to Steve Swallow with a look of disdain.

'You have vouched for him, so okay,' I said shaking my head.

Well let me tell you something about young Frank. He was born just outside of Glasgow but moved to Blackpool with his family as a youngster. He married young and has a few children and although he has the face of an angel he fights like the devil.

Frank is still a good friend of mine and I would have him backing me any time, any place. The last time I saw him he was wearing a bulletproof vest, so it doesn't look like too much has changed.

Joe Sweeney was from the same neck of the woods as Frank. He was a bit younger than me and he was an ex-Para. He was Frank's best friend and he was a one hundred per cent stand-up guy. Sadly Joe died a couple of years ago from the big C but he fought it to the end, typical of the man that he was.

For years the police in Blackpool had us down as an organised crime gang. We were constantly under surveillance and we were also questioned on crimes ranging from murder and armed robberies all the way down to jaywalking. It always made us laugh when a friendly policeman told us what crimes we were suspected of being involved in at that time. Organised crime? We were as organised as the group of lads in the film *Lock, Stock and Two Smoking Barrels* and if you have seen that film then you know how organised they were.

The trouble was that we were associating with proper old-school villains from one end of the country to the other and even over in Spain, so if any of them were under surveillance at the time that we were in their company, obviously the Old Bill or customs or whoever else might be carrying out the surveillance would want to know who we were, where we came from and what we might be up to. Once your name and face pops up, you are in their sights, and if it keeps popping up then you could be in a whole world of trouble that you don't even know you are in.

Through some of our contacts, we were introduced to some very shady people in London who we got on great with, both socially and in business dealings. We were soon travelling down to London so often that we ended up being nicknamed the 'Park Lane Boys' by the Cockneys we were associating with. This was because we always booked in at either the Park Lane Hilton or the Intercontinental on Park Lane, in a room that cost £200 a night even then. If there were more than three of us we would book a suite at £500 a night. We regularly frequented a couple of bars when we were down there, one of these being the Tin Pan Alley, run by Mad Frankie Fraser's nephew, and the other being a club in the West End by the name of Ferdenzies.

What a laugh we used to have there.

One night there was a few of us in the club but I had not seen Sharpie for some time. I checked with Frank Tonner and Joe Sweeney and neither of them had seen him for a short while. I checked with Petch, one of the London lads that we were out with. He said he had seen Ian going into the Gents about ten minutes ago. Thinking he might have gone for a toot, I went in after him. Entering the toilets, I could hear this slurred Blackpool accent saying, 'You cunts, coming to our town thinking you are the bee's knees.' Turning the corner, I found Ian growling at two cockneys backed up against a wall. I stood and listened for a few more seconds to make sure that the two London lads had not started on Ian in the first instance. But no, Ian, who was shitfaced, had come into the toilet and apparently had overheard these two blokes talking to each other about something that they had done or were going to do. Ian, thinking he was in Blackpool not London, decided to pull them. Realising that the two lads had not started anything with Sharpie, I intervened, explaining to Ian that we were in fact, at the present time, in London. We were in their neck of the woods. Ian just looked at me and then turned back to the two London lads, smiled with a big daft grin and said, 'Sorry'. With that he turned to me still smiling and asked me where I had been.

Petch, who had served ten years of a fourteen stretch for armed robbery, was introducing us to some proper people who needed some strange faces for a few little jobs. These involved fake customs ID cards and warrants and a fair bit of nerve. We were turning over shady cunts who were stashing large amounts of undeclared cash or ill-gotten gains. What you have to realise about these type of people is they just can't keep quiet about having a stash and there is always someone else who is greedy or jealous and willing to tell someone for a few quid. By the time they realised that they had been conned it was too late and anyway, who could they report it to? If they went to the Old Bill they would have to declare amounts of money or business dealings that they had been trying to keep quiet.

We ended up opening a safety deposit box where we could keep certain items and cash that we might need rather than transporting it up and down the motorway all the time. Things really got hairy when we were all nearly nabbed by an undercover police investigation that was nothing to do with what we were doing. The people that we were working with decided to call it a day for the time being and head for sunnier climates, and this suited us just fine.

One evening Ian and I were on our way back to Blackpool, having emptied the safe deposit box and closed our account. Ian was driving and I was having a snooze in the passenger seat. Opening my eyes to see where we were, I glanced over at the speedometer. We were travelling at a hundred miles an hour. I sat up quickly.

'Ian, what do you think will happen if we get pulled over by the police for speeding right now and the police decide to search the car?'

I could see the light come on in Ian's eyes as he realised the consequences and imagined a few possible scenarios. He soon slowed down to seventy miles an hour.

The pub was doing very well and I had managed to stay

off the police radar for a period of time, so everyone was happy – or so I thought. Martin, a good friend of mine who I had trained with for years, happened to be an armed response police officer in Blackpool. I had been on his stag do and to his wedding. Martin invited me to the police sports and social club that was located in the Blackpool Central police station. We met up and made our way to the social club on the ninth floor or thereabouts. We were soon having a good time, playing snooker with some of the other uniformed officers that were off duty.

I had noticed a couple of CID officers staring at me for a while. They did not seem very happy but I ignored them. They drank up and left the club, giving me a final dirty look. Within a matter of minutes a uniformed chief inspector came into the club. He looked around the room, which was quite large and was at that time fairly busy, and on seeing me he came over to the snooker table and asked who had signed me into the club. Martin stepped forward and said that he had.

Chief Inspector Rhodes then said to Martin, 'Get him out of here he is not welcome in this club and I will see you tomorrow.' With that he walked away. All the times they come and get me and take me to the police station against my will and then the first time I go voluntarily this happens. Now don't forget at this time I was a licensee of a town centre pub with just one spent conviction to my name from years before.

The next day Martin was kicked off the armed response unit and transferred to Preston. I was severely pissed off and threatened to take legal action if it would help Martin but he asked me to let it drop. It turned out that my picture was all over the CID room as target one in an on-going major investigation into an armed robbery.

It took Martin about twelve months before he man- aged to get reinstated to the armed response unit. Sorry pal. From that day on none of the uniforms that I considered myself to be friendly with were allowed to associate with me.

14

Party Time

A LOCAL BUSINESSMAN by the name of Parish Cobb came to see me at Promises. He was having trouble with an out-of-town security firm that was representing an ex-girlfriend of his. They were demanding a large amount of money from him or they would use physical violence. Parish was taking the threat seriously and he was very worried. He asked me if I would intervene on his behalf. We phoned the company, if I remember rightly they were called Century Security and they were from the Bolton area.

The man in charge of the company was a guy by the name of Belushi. Parish Cobb talked to him for a short time while I listened to the conversation, then I took the phone from Parish and introduced myself to this Belushi. Now this guy is one of those people that like to give it large when they are on the phone. He was telling me what he could do and how he would do it so in the end I gave him the address of the pub and invited him over to Blackpool to discuss it in person, face to face.

The next day I was contacted by a friend of mine named Tommy Houston. Tommy worked as a manager for Northern Security in Blackpool. Northern Security was the main supplier of door staff for licensed venues in the north-west of England and my own doormen, Scouse and John, were both employed by them. Tommy Houston asked me if I was having any problems, because a certain out-of-town security company had been on the phone to Northern Security asking about the strength of me, was I connected to any large firms and so on.

I asked Tommy what he had said to them.

'I told them the truth,' he said, 'that you were a dangerous bastard with a nice little firm.'

Parish Cobb turned up at Promises on a Friday afternoon, about a quarter of an hour before Belushi was supposed to turn up. He was very surprised to see that I was alone. To tell the truth so was I, as John Tate and Steve Warton should have been there by then. The club didn't open for another couple of hours so we were sat alone discussing how Parish wanted me to play it. The next minute there was a knock at the door.

Opening it, I thought it had gone dark early. The first man, who introduced himself as Belushi, was about the same size as me but the two blokes with him were fucking huge. They were blocking out the sunlight. Stepping aside, I let them past me into the club. Looking outside I could see they were by themselves, so I closed the door and turned around. Parish had gone white with the three men facing him.

I walked over and positioned myself in front of Parish.

'Right, you cunt,' I said. 'I know for a fact that you have phoned Northern Security asking about me, wanting to know what I can do, and you turn up with these two gorillas. Do you think that will frighten me, you prick?'

Then I pulled my trusty equaliser from the back of my trouser waistband and stuck it right in Belushi's mouth, not caring if I knocked out his teeth or not. I'll tell you what, those two big lumps could move. They covered the twenty feet to the fire doors in about a second and nearly knocked down a family walking by past the side exit.

Pushing Belushi back against the wall, I told Parish

Cobb to shut the door. I then proceeded to tell Belushi what I could do. To give him his due, he said to me, 'You are a big man with a gun in your hand.' Stepping back, I put the gun onto the bar and said to him, 'Party time, come on.' But he still bottled it then, so I fucked him off through the fire doors after his pals with his tail between his legs.

As I closed the doors, the phone started to ring. Walking over to it, I glanced across at Parish. He was standing there with a totally bemused expression on his face, unable to believe what he had witnessed. I answered the phone to find out it was a friend of mine named Jaconnelly, an old Glaswegian gangster. The conversation went something like this.

'Steve, it's Jaconnelly. I'm at the public phones outside British Home Stores, there are two blokes here that are phoning the police and screaming about a murder at Promises. Are you okay, mate?'

'Yes pal, no problems. Can you do me a favour? Walk past the club and take a parcel and keep it somewhere safe for me.'

'Aye, no worries pal.'

Jaconnelly was old school. He is dead now but he did me a massive favour that day and I will never forget him for that.

Twenty minutes later, I was in custody and had armed police searching my premises looking for a body. They were looking in the cellar and the kitchen, opening all the chest freezers. Obviously they didn't find one so I was released. Later that evening one of my staff called me over to take a telephone call.

'You took me by surprise this time but I will see you soon,' said this voice. Then he hung up on me.

'You fucking wanker!' I was spluttering and choking, I was that annoyed.

My good friend Steve Gibbo was still running the security at Mr Smith's nightclub in Warrington, so I phoned him and explained what had happened with this Belushi from Century Security. I asked him to phone Belushi's firm and pretend he needed some security for a special event and would it be possible for him to come across to Mr Smith's for a meeting.

Sure enough, one evening Belushi turned up at Mr Smith's as requested to meet Gibbo. Steve shook his hand and said, 'I would like you to meet an associate of mine before we discuss any business,' and led him to a secluded office. It was like something from out of a film: I was in a swivel chair with my back to the door, Steve Warton was sat on the edge of the desk and Belushi must have assumed it was him he was to meet.

Steve Warton shook his head and said to him, 'No it's not me, it's this Steve.' With that I span around in the chair. When he recognised me he nearly started crying.

'My wife is in the car, I'm sorry, please, I'm sorry, my wife is in the car.' He went to pieces. He must have thought I was going to kill him.

I stood up and walked around the desk to face him.

'This is how easy it is. If I get any more silly phone calls after tonight I will find you and bury you, you dick.'

With that we let him leave the club and I am pleased to say that I have never heard from him again.

I was approached by a couple of ladies to see if I would be interested in hosting an Ann Summers evening on a quiet early week night. At that time I was not too sure what this consisted of, but once I found out I thought it would be a bit of a laugh. I was very surprised when the organisers told me that they had sold nearly three hundred tickets. Then came the bombshell: the ladies did not want any male staff to be working. I explained to them that this was not possible, Jimmy the Dancer was the disc jockey and Scouse and John were the security and I would have to oversee everything. They were not very happy about this until I came up with a solution: any male staff working that night would work in drag, dressed up as women. Now this was a couple of years before the Funny Girls transvestite bar opened up in Blackpool but there were still plenty of gay nightclubs.

Well, the security lads were not very happy about standing on the door in drag but I sweetened it by giving them an extra few quid. Jimmy the Dancer just worried about colour coding and what accessories he should have. I had the biggest problem finding some clothes to fit me. In the end I managed to get an all-in-one – very nice, but a little tight if you know what I mean – and a skirt, combined with a wavy blonde wig and trainers. I think I looked quite fetching. Jimmy the Dancer looked amazing in one of his girlfriend's dresses (see photo section).

The night was a huge success with only a slight hiccup. A group of squaddies from the army camp at Weeton, a few miles outside Blackpool, tried gate-crashing the door. The doormen called for me and when I attended the door the soldiers started saying that they fought for us and that we should look after them. I explained to them that no-one fights for us, we fight our own battles. With that it kicked off good style, spilling out into the street.

A passer-by or a CCTV operator apparently reported it to the police by telephone, with the report saying something like this: 'There is a disturbance outside Promises nightclub. A large female is battering a group of men.' By the time the police attended it was all over. No-one was seriously hurt, the only thing really hurt was the soldiers' pride. We were not willing to press any charges and the soldiers definitely did not want to. I won't say what regiment they were from but this was not the British fighting man at his best.

The Ann Summers evening was a major success for the organisers and for my takings. We also regularly gave to, or held events for, charities. One day Peter McCarthy, who was working for me, came up with the idea of getting a group together to do a parachute jump for charity. We did the training over the weekend for the jump to take place on the Sunday morning at the Black Knights Parachute Centre in Cockerham, Lancashire.

For whatever reason, most of the people in the party that was taking part in the jump the next morning stayed at Promises on the Saturday night on the piss. A lot of them were also on charlie and ecstasy. When we were all being kitted up for the jump we saw a big sign that said, 'No alcohol or drugs to be taken before taking part in a parachute jump.' Looking at the state of some of our group, I would not have been surprised if some of them had floated upwards when they jumped from the plane, not fallen down towards the earth, they were that high on gear.

I was to be on the first plane with three other jumpers, Steve Warton, Dave Garside and Steve Daley. There were also the pilot and the jump master. The perfectly good plane that we were going to throw ourselves out of was not very big but we all managed to get into our allotted positions. I was going to be the first to jump and was looking forward to it. The plane thundered down the runway with the wind streaming in to buffet us.

We all kept looking around nervously at each other as the plane failed to take off. All of a sudden the pilot cut back on the throttle and slowed the plane to a crawl and then turned it and headed back to where we had all climbed aboard in the first place. When the engine stopped the jump master told us that we were far too heavy and that two of us would have to swap with two smaller people from the second four. Bollocks!

Seeing as how I was going to be the first one out, I was the first to be changed. Steve Daley floated off and landed somewhere near Lancaster and then he had to walk about three or four miles to get back to the jump site carrying his parachute.

A couple of lads ended up hanging from trees and a girl named Carmen broke her leg and then very nearly drowned as she was dragged into a ditch full of water. Pete and I were her rescuers; I later visited her in hospital and gave her a cherry paratrooper's beret. Another jumper also broke his leg. Despite the injuries, everyone that could then went back to Promises and the party continued. All in all it was a good day and we raised about £3,000 for charity.

There were many good times like that. But the nature of the business I was in, and of the reputation I had, meant the prospect of serious violence was never far away.

Mark McGovern, affectionately known to some as 'Mr Magoo', was in the music promotions business. He had helped Ian Sharples at his club Shaboo by getting him some top DJs and guest artists. Magoo also ran a rave night at a club on the Central Pier in Blackpool called Oz. This was the club that I had worked at many years before when it was called the Dixieland. Over the years it had undergone many alterations.

Ian was at the club with Magoo when some young lads started to get a bit naughty. Ian stepped forward to have a word with these lads, who were all about nineteen years old, to tell them to behave themselves and one of them decided to have a pop at him. The lad threw a couple of punches at Ian but they lacked any real power. Ian slapped the kid once and he went down. All the usual verbal bullshit followed: 'You don't know who you are dealing with, you dickhead', 'You are dead, you cunt', and all that bollocks.

The following Friday night at about eleven o'clock, Sharpie, Frank, Joe and myself were all in Oz having a drink with Magoo when one of the doormen came flying through the crowd as if he was being chased by the devil himself. There were a large number of men, possibly as many as fifty, outside and one of them was asking for Magoo by name.

The man asking for Mark was a local hotelier named Tony Raynor. Tony, who was originally from Manchester, was well known around the town and had a lot of associates in common with us. He owned a couple of hotels in the town centre.

I went to the door with Joe Sweeney. Walking down the stairs to the door, I saw Tony Raynor's lips move. I visualised my name being spoken to the man looking at me. 'Open the door,' I said to the two doormen, who were visibly shaking with fear. I stood to the side to let Tony and the man he was talking to through the entrance, along with two other men who looked like they could be brothers.

The man and the group that were with him hailed from Middleton, near Manchester. The man that Tony Raynor was speaking to was David Ward, a well-known Manchester heavy, and the group with him were his firm. David Ward is a stocky man with dark hair. He stands about five feet ten inches tall and is a former professional boxer. You can see he is confident in his own ability.

Just as I was shaking hands with Dave, Joe Sweeney began swapping punches with one of the other two men that had entered the club with him. Here we go, I thought. At the same time I was curious to know what it was all about. Dave Ward told two men with him to 'calm down'.

Magoo finally arrived at the scene and decided to let the full group in. It turned out that the young lad that Ian Sharples had slapped the week before was David Ward's nephew and they wanted to have a word with him. Oh well, Sharpie does it again.

Looking at this crew as they were filing past us I could tell that some of them, if not all, were tooled up.

Jimmy the Dancer had just arrived from Promises to bring me something and came straight over to me.

'What's going on?' he asked, looking at the Middleton lads.

After a quick explanation, I asked him if he had transport, because I knew he could not drive. He told me that one of his friends was outside with a car. I looked him straight in the eye and asked him if he was willing to go and collect our guns and bring them to us at the club right now. Knowing how precarious the situation was at that time, Jimmy did not hesitate. Now Jimmy has his faults just like everyone else but you have to admit that is the type of person you want working for you.

There were no mobile phones in those days but within ten minutes or so local faces began to turn up asking us if everything was all right. Stephen Hill, the boss of the security firm that was on the door, even turned up with his back-up bus, a people carrier full of doormen that would travel around town waiting for an incident at one of their venues.

Jimmy returned with our peacemakers, which made me feel a whole lot better. We had managed to keep Ian out of the way until we were prepared to face the odds against us. I still don't know to this day if the Manchester lads had sussed out that we were carrying shooters by then, but when Ian sat down at the table with Dave Ward and his brothers, everything went well.

The next thing, it kicked off in the toilets. Again I thought, *here it goes*, but no, it was down to customers that had nothing to do with either party. The atmosphere in the club was still very tense and the best way to calm things down as far as I was concerned was for us to fuck off back to Promises. We had stayed there long enough without incident. Any longer might lead to an unnecessary confrontation that could escalate out of control.

The four of us returned to Promises. When it closed, instead of allowing people to stay behind like I usually did on a Friday or Saturday night, I cleared the place.

Sitting there drinking alcohol along with the odd line of charlie did not put us in the ideal relaxation mode. Instead, the more we thought about it the more wound up and excitable we became. There is a fantastic advertising campaign on the television and radio about people feeling invulnerable when they have drunk a certain amount of alcohol. *This is our town and they have come here team-handed, cheeky twats! Who do they think they are dealing with?* All that bollocks started coming out.

Alcohol and drugs really can get you in a whole new world of trouble and pain.

At three or four o'clock in the morning we decided to go to Tony Raynor's hotel, the Buxton Manor on Albert Road. That is where they should all be if they had booked in for the night or stayed behind for a drink. When we arrived at the Buxton Manor it was in darkness and we had to knock at the door. The door was answered by a big man that none of us knew. He was quite aggressive and ended up getting knocked on his arse. When he was on the ground some-one decided to put a bullet between his legs to show him how different it could have been for him, which was not a very good idea considering the time and the place. Lights started to go on everywhere so we decided to get back to the safety of my venue rather quickly before the police turned up at the hotel.

All this activity did nothing to calm us down, in fact if anything it made us worse. We were very agitated by then and led ourselves to believe that they would come for us. They knew where we could be found and so they could pick any time that suited them.

As I say, alcohol and drugs can get you into a whole heap of trouble. We came to the conclusion that we would take it to them first. How do we find them?

The answer: Tony Raynor. He brought them to Oz, the club on the pier, so he should know where they lived or socialised. We could kidnap him and make him take us there. The four of us loaded up with weapons, money and passports and drove to Tony's house near St Annes.

You should have seen his face when we turned up at his house and let him into our little plan. He swore blind that Dave Ward and his firm had no intention of carrying anything on; in fact, if we would let him, he would phone him now and I could speak to him myself.

When I spoke to Dave on the phone he confirmed what Tony Raynor had been telling us. As far as he was concerned he had to back his nephew up to a certain degree, which he had done by a show of force. They were quite happy with the way Ian Sharples had explained what had happened with Dave's nephew the previous week and why it had happened. The incident at the Buxton Manor was not mentioned which was especially good news for us.

Shortly after this incident, Dave Ward received a twelve-stretch at Her Majesty's pleasure for kidnapping and torturing a rival. Dave could probably write his own book about his experiences if he is able to mention them without incriminating himself.

Then a couple of years ago, a good friend of mine named Paul Kirby and I went to a hotel in Blackpool for a late-night drink. As I was standing at the bar, in a room full of rough-looking blokes, I noticed some of the group kept looking at me and talking amongst themselves. As one of them got up and walked over to me, I once again thought, here we fucking go.

He had a puzzled look on his face as he approached.

'Excuse me mate, are you Steve Sinclair?' he asked, quite amicably.

Looking over the guy's shoulder I saw that all his mates were still sat down so I didn't think it was trouble he was after. Standing up straight, I nodded and said, 'Yes, I'm Steve Sinclair. Why, who are you?'

It turned out to be some of the Middleton crew who

were in Blackpool for the night.

'Dave is upstairs in his room, come on up, he will be pleased to see you.'

I went up to the room and sure enough Dave was there. He had not long been released from prison and he was genuinely pleased to see me.

I have bumped into Dave and some of his crew on a few occasions since then at unexpected times and in unexpected places. He still comes over to Blackpool every now and again, so in hindsight we had a very good result that night. All the best mate.

15

Too Quiet

IN 1992, ALTHOUGH the pub was doing quite well, I received news from the company I worked for that they had decided to downsize and were putting Promises on the market. They were willing to offer me first refusal. The price that they wanted for the lease – not even the freehold – was £80,000. Where the fuck was I going to get £80,000 from? To top it all, the rent plus VAT worked out at £1,300 a week.

I talked to a few people to see if there was any interest at this price or even if it was a viable project. The premises is a licensed, three-storey building right in the town centre with a very large cellar underneath. The ground floor was the pub/nightclub, the first floor was empty and had not been used for quite a few years, while the top floor was very spacious living accommodation. After doing a business plan, we worked out that it would be viable if we could knock the asking price down by more than a few thousand pounds to somewhere near the £50,000 mark. I talked to the owner of the company and we agreed a price. That was the good news. The bad news was that we still needed a large amount of money.

A good friend of mine offered to come in with some serious money. This enabled me to register my own company, purchased off the shelf from Companies

House. It was called Ploughmear Ltd. I was the director and Tanee was the company secretary.

Everything seemed to be going in our favour for a short time, but fate dealt us a crap hand. My pal who lent me the money suffered a serious financial loss and desperately needed the money that he had lent me back as soon as possible, otherwise he faced bankruptcy. I approached a few banks to see if there was any chance of raising the cash but there was no chance in the limited time available to us. I am not a religious person and I have never professed to be but I was in a situation that I had no control over and I may have thrown in a few quick prayers for the man upstairs just for good measure to see if anyone was listening. I was really worried for my friend.

As if someone had heard a prayer, word was passed through to me that there was an out-of-town firm in Blackpool flashing a load of cash that had allegedly come from a drug deal they had just done. If that was true, they would not be able to go to the Old Bill if anything happened to their money, would they? The rest, as they say, is history. I carried on as the new leaseholder of Promises and my friend's financial problems were sorted out satisfactorily.

Not long after this event, one Saturday evening in Promises, Jimmy the Dancer approached me to say that there was a Scouser in the club selling drugs. Once I had identified the person in question, I watched him for a while. Sure enough he was dealing. Pulling him in to the disabled toilets, I asked him what the fuck he thought he was doing selling drugs in my club. Instead of apologising he got cheeky, so I gave him a slap and then got him to empty his pockets. He had some ecstasy tablets and about £100 in cash in his pocket. He also had a big wad of cash hidden in the lining of his jacket.

He started getting leery again, trying to tell me that I did not know who I was dealing with. Giving him another slap, I took the big wad of cash from him and threw him out of the club. He was screaming at me, 'I'll fucking shoot you, you are fucking dead,' all the usual crap.

The next thing I knew, the police were at the door asking for me. There were two uniformed coppers and this Scouse cunt at the door. My mind was going ten to the dozen.

One of the policemen motioned to me to step out and to the side of the door.

'Steve, this man has made an allegation of theft against you. He claims you have taken all his money from him and thrown him out of the club. Is this true?'

I am looking this Scouse cunt right in the eye as the copper was talking to me. He is actually smirking at me. I feel like stamping all over his face.

Then I noticed that one of his trouser pockets was bulging out. It was my turn to smirk.

'No,' I reply. 'I threw him out after seeing him offering drugs for sale. When I searched him he had about one hundred pounds in his trouser pockets and some tablets. I bet he still has it on him.'

Well his face was a picture. When the police officer turned to him and asked him to empty his pockets, there was the money that I had not taken from him. *Result*. It just goes to show that it can pay you not to be too greedy.

Talking of being too greedy, I had to let Jimmy D go because I found out he had been watering down the stock. It was a shame because he was having a bit of a hard time in some other matters. I am pleased to say that we are still very good friends to this day, Jimmy turned his life around and has a lovely family of his own now.

With the club being right in the town centre it seemed a bit silly for it to be closed during the day, what with all the lunchtime trade we were missing. After checking that the licence enabled us to, we decided to brighten the place up and open at lunchtimes. Soon things were going well: perhaps too well. Obviously I should have

been worried with it being too quiet. A local would-be gangster that had just got out of prison by the name of Tommy H came into Promises and tried throwing his weight about. I took the lad downstairs into the cellar for a quiet chat and when that didn't work I ended up giving the cunt a slap.

'Get rid of that piece of shit,' I said to big Stuart 'Iron Balls' Jackson, who was the doorman at that time. Stuart soon came flying back up the stairs.

'Steve, can I have a word?' he asked, motioning me to the back. 'That piece of shit is dead,' he whispered.

Fuck, fuck, fuck. I knew it had been too quiet. Running down the stairs, I was thinking, *what the fuck can I do with the body when the club upstairs is heaving?* I spotted the big chest freezer that stood off to one side of the cellar.

'Help me put him in here for now,' I said to Stuart, lifting the lid.

Pointing at H's feet, I grabbed hold of his shoulders. As I heaved him up, he only went and groaned.

'You cunt,' I shouted at Stuart. 'He's not fucking dead.' Then, realising what I had said, I said it again, this time with genuine relief: 'He's not dead!'

We ended up putting him in a shop doorway and phoning an ambulance. Thankfully the council didn't have CCTV up then. The cunt made a full recovery and ended up getting another slap from me some time later. He is still a dickhead to this day, and the last I heard was facing a firearms charge.

Sharpie was in trouble again. He had gone on holiday with a group of lads. Although he knew them from his old club, he wasn't that close to them. Once they were settled in to their hotel in Ayia Napa, Cyprus, they had hired a jeep and all piled onto it. A few hours later the driver crashed and a few of the group sustained minor injuries. While the group of Blackpool lads were at the hospital, one of them dropped a plastic straw that had been cut down to about three inches in length from his pocket.

A sharp-eyed Cypriot police officer attending the hospital because of the crash spotted the straw and took possession of it. He noticed traces of a white powder on the straw and immediately called for back-up from the drug squad. The individual who had dropped it was searched and arrested and then their hotel was turned over by the police. Guess what? It was all over the Cyprus national paper: the first ecstasy tablets ever found on the island. I am not sure how much the police found but there was ecstasy, cocaine and some weed. Ian ended up taking the collar for the full group.

I was in Promises when the news got back to me. The rest of the group Ian had travelled with had just come home and left him there. I went fucking mad. After I had had a word or two with a few of them, I booked a flight to Cyprus. Stuart Jackson, a top geezer by anyone's standards, said he would come with me.

I looked at my watch. It was nearly six o'clock in the morning and the club was still full of people. It had been a good night with plenty of money going across the bar and when the customers were spending I would often let them have a lock-in. Then I remembered something. The flight from Manchester Airport to Paphos was leaving at about eleven in the morning, meaning we had to be at the airport at approximately eight o'clock. Fuck! Kicking everyone out, including Stuart Jackson, who had to go home and pack, I got my passport and travel things together in a hurry, just as my lift turned up.

By the time we had settled into our hotel in Paphos and then hired a jeep it was nearly ten o'clock at night local time, but we drove straight through to Larnaca over a hundred miles away and more by luck than by judgement we found the police station where Ian was being held.

When we asked in English if they had an Ian Sharples in custody, the police officer at the desk looked at the size of Stuart and myself and, judging by the look on his face, he must have thought we had come to break Ian out.

Ian was due in court the next morning so Stuart and I decided to stay in Larnaca that night and give him some moral support. The day before we had left Blackpool we had bought two light blue *Thunderbirds* caps ('International Rescue') from a stall on Blackpool promenade.

Cyprus is a United Nations base and any military forces operating for the UN wear light blue berets or caps. When we entered the court building, we put on these caps even though we were in civilian clothes. On entering the courtroom where Ian was being tried, but where the judge was not yet present, I hummed the *Thunderbirds* theme tune. Everyone in the room, including Sharpie, turned around to look. Seeing us with these caps on, Ian just put his head in his hands. I still don't know if he was laughing or crying.

Anyway, it didn't work. He got sent down. The judge kept saying 'six months for this' and 'six months for that'. I nearly had to take my shoes off to add them all up as I had run out of fingers, even using Stuart's as well as my own. Luckily for Ian, when he finished going through the separate sentences he said the magic word 'concurrent'. Thank fuck for that. In the end he would only have to serve six months.

He was sent to the 'Nicosia Hilton', where he did time with lifers, terrorists and holidaymakers who had been a little bit naughty. One of the terrorists serving a life sentence there was an English bloke called Ian Davidson, who did a job for the Palestinian Liberation Organisation in Cyprus against an Israeli target, killing three Jewish tourists on a yacht in Larnaca marina. It was shown on international television news programmes all around the world. My mate Ian reckoned he was a nice geezer once you got to know him. I ended up going out to Cyprus every month to visit him. Well, what are friends for?

One of the visits nearly went tits up for us from the first night. Steve Daley and I had arrived at the Poseidon Hotel in Limassol. We decided to go for a few drinks before turning in for the night so as to have an early start the next day. After a couple of hours we were both off our heads and I ended up having a bit of an argument with some taxi drivers who, according to the manager of the bar we were in, were supposed to be part of the local mafia.

Now I am a big man but Steve Daley, although a bit shorter, is a lot more muscular than me. As soon as Steve saw me with these guys, outside he came, barrelling through the crowd and pushing a couple of men away from me just as two Cypriot policemen arrived. Without asking any questions, they arrested Steve. They soon had him in handcuffs but struggled to get him into the back of their car. One of the coppers then punched Steve in the side of the head but Steve didn't even notice it, thank God. I had melted into the crowd at the first sign of the police but as soon as the punch landed on the side of Steve's head I put myself back in the frame with all the usual bollocks.

'Whoah, there's no need for any of that.'

Steve was taken to the Limassol police station which was only over the road, so I went as well. Once we were all inside the station, things deteriorated quickly. Steve was still handcuffed and the coppers were becoming very physical. I ended up putting one of them on the floor and holding him there by his throat. One of the other policemen then picked up a chair to hit me with, so Steve shoulder-barged him into the wall. They came out with the CS gas and down we both went.

We were both whimpering like schoolgirls on our hands and knees; all the fight had gone out of us. Then the bastards made a mistake: they started laying into us with batons. After taking about four strikes across my back and head, rage must have taken away the pain from the gas, because I roared like a wounded bear and surged upright. I grabbed one of the coppers just as he was swinging his baton at me and threw him over a desk. Steve was also up and screaming at the coppers, 'Come on you cunts, is that the best you can do?' I picked up a baton that one of them had dropped and we backed up against a wall. The disturbance had obviously alerted the rest of the station because a policeman came running into the room carrying a gun in his hand. He turned out to be the senior officer in charge and he spoke very good English, thank fuck.

After a bit of shouting, mainly him telling me to drop the baton, I replied, 'Either get the British consulate down here and charge us or we will apologise and you can let us go.'

Steve Daley looked at me and said, 'Eh?' as if to say, where the fuck did that come from? I looked at him and said, 'Duh, fuck knows.'

The senior officer looked at his men, who were all over on the other side of the room and then at the state of us. We were cut and bleeding and we had been CS gassed but it was obvious that we were pissed off and felt that we had been mistreated. Now we don't know if those policemen that had arrested Steve had a habit of abusing holidaymakers or not but the head man said, 'You will apologise.'

Steve and I looked at each other and both nodded our heads, 'Yes, yes, of course we will.' He then spoke to his officers in Greek. When he finished he turned back to us and, putting away his gun, said with a big smile, 'We have coffee and brandy.' Then he pointed at the policeman that had started it all and said his name and that he would drive us back to our hotel. To this day, Steve Daley and I still don't understand why it turned out the way it did but if it had gone the other way we would have both probably got longer than Sharpie.

It took us a couple of days before we were able to move well enough to hire a car and drive through to see Ian at Nicosia prison. When we told him what had happened, he said, 'How the fuck can you get away with something like that and I get nicked for a bit of gear?'

The first night we were fit enough to go out for a drink again we ended up in the same bar where it had all started. The bar was deserted apart from us and the manager-owner, a cockney Cypriot. We were sat talking about what had occurred the other night. It had apparently become common knowledge along the Limassol nightclub strip.

A man came in, bought a small beer and sat right next to me. I asked the manager if he knew him at all. He didn't so I asked the man if he would move a bit further away from me. He ignored me so I asked him again with no effect. Picking up his beer, I said to him, 'You are either a queer or a copper and I don't want you sat next to me, now fuck off!' With that, I poured his beer over his head. He stood up and looked at me, not knowing what to do. Then he showed us his warrant card. I was right. I thought it would all kick off again but he just left the club with a disgusted look on his face. I could not wait to get off that island.

Frank Tonner and Joseph Sweeney made up the other half of our little firm and they would get up to their own little adventures and do their own jobs on the side, the same as Ian Sharples and I would. Ian was banged up in Cyprus which left the three of us, or so I thought. It was on a Friday or Saturday evening as Frank and Joe, who were now the security at Promises, opened the club doors that everything went a bit wobbly.

As I was stood with the two of them at the door, a bomber taxi pulled up outside the club with a group of men in it. The driver got out from the cab and opened the rear door. As soon as all the party had exited the taxi, they and the driver, plus a couple of other men who had appeared to be walking past the door, all jumped on Frank and Joe. As I went to help them, one or more of the men pulled warrant cards from their pockets and shouted, 'We are police officers, stay out of it Sinclair, we just want these two.'

Then I heard one of the men reading Frank and Joe their rights and also saying that they were being arrested on suspicion of supplying class A drugs. *Fuck me*, I thought, *that's all I need* (I meant them being arrested, not that I needed some class A drugs; mind you, come to think of it ...). Apparently they had both been active in supplying cocaine and one of their contacts had been busted in possession of quite a large amount of charlie and immediately told the police who it belonged to. Both Frank and Joe were ultimately sent down for a few years apiece. So that was how I came to be Billy No-Mates for a while.

My dad said to me one day, 'If I ever catch you doing cocaine, Steve, I will rub your nose in it.' Top man, my dad.

A funny thing happened when they were both in Preston Prison. I visited them and was told about another prisoner from the Manchester area who was also on remand at the time. He had told them a story about how he had come to be arrested in Blackpool. He had booked in to a bed and breakfast hotel in the North Shore area. He had allegedly brought a large quantity of cocaine to sell in a deal to someone in the Blackpool area but he had been arrested before the deal had been completed.

He had told Frank and Joe that he had stashed a load of cocaine and some money under the carpet in his room at the hotel. He also said to Frank and Joe that the police had never mentioned this at any time.

You can probably guess as to what happened next, or

should I say what you think happened next. The lads managed to get the name of the hotel from the kid. It was just off Gynn Square but they could not get the room number. All they knew was that it was a single room on the first floor. That shouldn't be too hard to find, should it?

I booked into the hotel under an assumed name saying that a friend of mine had recommended it to me. Apparently he had stayed in a lovely single room on the first floor.

'Oh, it will have been one of a choice of three,' said the landlady, smiling politely.

Fuck!

After two more visits to try all the rooms and plenty of 'Are you sure you are okay in there?' from the landlady when she could hear the furniture being moved around throughout my stay, I found sweet fuck all. Oh well, you win some, you lose some. I'm not sure if Frank and Joe gave the lad who had told them the story a good hiding or not but I would have if I could have caught up with him. Saying that, the cleaners or even the sweet little landlady might have already found it before I got there.

Things were going very well for us at this time so I thought it might be a good time for a family holiday. My mum and dad had never been able to afford to take us abroad as a family but they had always made sure that we enjoyed ourselves when we were kids. They used to take us for bike rides and swimming as often as possible. I don't know if it was to tire us out during the school holidays or not but they were good times that I remember with affection.

I decided to give them a surprise and treat them to a cruise on the *Queen Elizabeth 2* with Tanee, Christie and me. I booked a trip that entailed us having two nights in

New York, giving us time to have a good look around the city sights before we joined the ship for a transatlantic crossing back to Southampton. I made arrangements for my friend Steve Swallow to look after the boozer for me. Steve was having problems at home, so he was only too happy to have the chance to get away from the marital home for a while.

The day for the holiday finally came around and we were checking in at the ticket desk at Manchester Airport. They took our tickets and passports from us and started messing with their computers.

'Mr Sinclair,' said the young lady behind the desk, 'there seems to be a problem.'

Now my mum and dad had been a bit unsure about the whole thing and Tanee was downright scared to death about the flight, so this 'we seem to have a problem' nearly sent me over the edge. The only one who was not bothered about anything was Christie in her pushchair, who as an infant did not have a clue anyway.

They had fully booked the economy section of the aircraft but had assumed that two Mr and Mrs Sinclairs were an error and let the extra two seats be sold off. They only went and put my mum and dad in first class; not me, who was paying for everything, and Tanee, but my mum and dad. Well, my old man was like the cat with the cream. He kept sending bits of food and drink back to the peasants and he was winding me up like you would a broken clock. My mum must have realised that I was getting wound up even though I was very happy for them. She came through to the economy section and sat with Tanee and Christie whilst I went forward to the first class section and sat with my dad.

We had a couple of free days in New York City before the *Queen Elizabeth* was due to dock and it was a treat for all of us. The morning of the day that we were to join the ship came but so did some stunning news. The *QE2* had run onto a sandbank and sustained some damage so the cruise was off and everybody had to pack and fly back home instead. To say that we were unhappy would be a slight understatement. Poor Tanee, who had only agreed to the trip because we only had to fly one way, was distraught.

On our return to Blackpool, I was surprised to find that Steve Swallow, who had offered to look after the place for me while I was away, was in hospital. What the fuck had happened now? It turned out that Steve had been running the place for a couple of days with no problems, but he was well aware of some of my previous escapades and realised that there might be some comebacks from certain people. On this particular day, the club was open for business downstairs and Steve was just getting ready to go down. As he was leaving the lounge, he said he felt a searing pain in his stomach causing him to collapse on to the floor.

The flat above Promises was overlooked at the front by the council-owned West Street car park. Steve thought that someone had shot him from there, thinking that he was me. He tried to get up but could not stand, the pain was too intense, so he dragged himself down the hall.

To get out of the flat he had to pass Thumper. Now Thumper is a big, daft, friendly bull mastiff who liked Swallow. In fact he liked Swallow so much he decided he wanted to give him one. Every time Swallow tried to crawl past him to get out of the flat and get help, Thumper would drag him back to try and hump him.

Can you imagine how much I was laughing when Steve was telling me this?

In the end Swallow had to wait until Thumper had tired himself out enough so that he could escape. By this time Barbara, my friend Robin Thompson's mother, who was the cashier on the door at the time, was wondering where Steve was. She found him on the stairs and immediately called an ambulance. It turned out that Steve had suffered a burst ulcer and could have died if Thumper had lasted any longer. Well I was in stitches and so was Steve Swallow, literally.

Cunard compensated the passengers that missed the trip by offering either a refund or another cruise. Tanee, Christie and I went on a cruise to the Norwegian fjords on the *QE2* the following year and we were upgraded to first class on the ship. Sadly my mum and dad were not able to come with us but I gave them the money instead, which came in useful for them in their retirement.

16

The Law of the Blade

A NICE PEACEFUL Saturday evening at Promises was shattered when news came through to me about an incident that had just happened at the Le Cage nightclub on Topping Street. Michael Creasy, my old boxing buddy, was running the security there. His head doorman was Glen Lawson, who had worked with me at Just Ji's. Two men had been refused entry to the club at the front door. One of these men was well-known in the Blackpool area for being involved in the drug scene, the other one was a stranger to the doormen but it had been noted that both were Scottish.

Now Glen himself is from Scotland and he knew the local man quite well. I am not certain what was said at the time but a short while later Glen and another man named Harry Gunn were outside by the back door having a quiet smoke when a car pulled up. A man jumped out of the passenger side of the car and without saying anything set about Glen and Harry, stabbing both men repeatedly. The man then jumped back into the car and it sped off.

Mick Creasy contacted me at Promises to tell me he knew the identity of one of the men involved in the incident. The man that he knew I will call Rolo; this is not his proper name but it is close enough. I knew him too, in fact I got on quite well with him. He was with a lad from Scotland by the name of McCracken who was supposedly on the run for attempted murder in Glasgow. I might have known Rolo but he or the man with him had stabbed one of my pals and, as the saying goes, someone had to pay the piper.

I met up with Mick and heard the full story. He was obviously very annoyed about what had happened to one of his men and wanted some payback. He wanted to know if I would go with him to have a word with these cunts. I said of course I would go with him. I don't like people who use knives at the best of times but Glen is also a good pal of mine, so there was no hesitation as far as I was concerned.

We knew where Rolo was staying at the time. This was in a ground floor flat in the North Shore, known as bedsit land. When we arrived at the address, I got a baseball bat from the boot of my car. Mick asked me what I was doing and why was I using a bat, we were both big strong men with reputations for being able to fight with our fists. Mick is like that, straight as a die but a bit naïve when it came to situations like this.

'Michael, one of those two cunts in there has just repeatedly stabbed two unarmed men. If you think I am going to grapple with someone who is carrying a knife you have got another thing coming. He can have this bat round his fucking head.'

We pressed the door bell and waited. After a few seconds a young woman came to the front door. As soon as she opened it we were through into a hallway, pushing her to one side. I saw an open flat door and headed for it. She started to scream, shouting Rolo's name, so I knew we were heading for the right flat.

Before we reached it, the door slammed shut. They were probably nervous about what had happened earlier and someone must have been stood by the door waiting to see who it was. I heard a male shouting something from inside the flat, so I decided not to stop and hit the door with my shoulder. The door came off the frame and travelled in front of me into a corridor. That door saved my life. A young man of about twenty-two, who I did not recognise, swung a meat cleaver at me. It hit the door right next to my head with a solid thud.

As the man struggled to free the cleaver, I introduced him to the baseball bat.

Rolo, who has a bad leg as the result of a car crash, was off through the door and past Mick like a white Linford Christie. I saw Mick look at the meat cleaver that the other cunt had tried to hit me with. He shook his head and took off after Rolo.

I twatted my new best pal off all the walls inside the small flat, to the chorus of two women screaming at me to leave him alone. Leave him alone? I wanted to cave his head in.

McCracken was soon lying on the floor with blood coming from various places about his head. I looked at him and then I looked at the meat cleaver that was in the hall. Walking across the room, I bent down and picked it up and, leaving my baseball bat by the door, I returned to McCracken. I squatted next to him.

'McCracken, look at me you cunt. Look at me.'

When he opened his eyes, I raised the cleaver above my head and said, 'Let's see how you like it.'

I buried the cleaver into the floor as close as I could next to his head.

'Tell him to fuck off back to Scotland, it's safer for him.'

I stood up and started to walk out of the flat, picking up the bat. I looked back. McCracken had not moved and the two women were looking at me with hatred in their eyes. Fuck them. I turned back into the room and pulled the cleaver from the floor. The girls gasped, probably thinking I had decided to do McCracken with it after all, but I just used my jacket to wipe my prints from the handle and then dropped it back onto the floor.

Leaving the flat, I met up with Mick Creasy, who had finally caught the fleeing Rolo and given him a good hiding in the street.

'Fucking hell Steve, I'm glad I am not into that game,' he said to me, looking at the bat but probably visualising the cleaver hitting the door next to my head.

I am pleased to say that Glen Lawson and Harry Gunn both made a full recovery and suffered no lasting injuries.

The unlikely venue of the Academy Club, on Union Street, Plymouth, was where I very nearly came to an untimely end. The reason I was there, more than three hundred miles from my manor, was because my good friend Graham Blow had invested a lot of cash into buying and doing up the Academy, then the largest club in Plymouth. When I say a large investment, I am talking about hundreds of thousands of pounds. The club was having a hard time of it and Graham believed a lot of the problems were because of a certain gang of locals, led by an individual named Martin Kenny. Graham believed this gang were responsible for the drugs that were being brought into the club and also some violent attacks and intimidation on his door staff.

I had been down to Plymouth with Graham when he was first thinking about buying the Academy. We had come down to the naval dockyard city on the south coast on a Friday so we could get the feel of how the locals enjoyed their weekends. Graham had asked me to go with him because he thought that, with me being brought up in Portsmouth, another naval dockyard city, I might have a good idea what it would be like.

Graham was sure that some of his door staff were involved with this gang. Obviously he was right to some extent, as Kenny and his firm came in that night and they already knew that Graham had brought someone in. I was walking through the club with Pete Flackett, who was down in Plymouth doing some building work for Graham, when we were confronted by this group of about ten men. Talking obviously did not work because everything soon went tits up. I ended up being stabbed in the left thigh and the left buttock. I was also bottled numerous times to the head, leaving me requiring about sixty stitches, some to stop an arterial bleed. Pete Flackett suffered a broken arm and severe bruising to most of his body.

When I finally came out of the operating theatre, the Plymouth Regional Crime Squad were waiting to question me on suspected firearms offences. They alleged that when it had kicked off in the club, I had got into it with Martin Kenny but was hit with a bottle from the side. I had then grabbed hold of Kenny and pulled him in close to try to stop the others from attacking me any further. They then said I had pulled a gun from my inside jacket pocket, stuck it in Martin's throat and told him to tell them to back off or I would blow his head off. When they had all backed off, and I had allegedly let Kenny go, the full gang all then ran out of the club.

Imagine if the alleged gun had gone off accidentally. I would have had to go into hiding rather than be taken to the hospital. If that had been the case I would probably have bled to death.

The Regional Crime Squad searched my hotel room but did not find anything that was incriminating. They also phoned through to the Blackpool police for information on me and they were told by some wise-ass Lancashire copper that it would be like the AA: someone would turn up in the middle of the night, fix it and then fuck off. Cheeky bastards. I don't know where they get that impression of me.

That was probably the worst beating I had ever taken and I have taken a few over the years. The matter rested there and I later heard Kenny went down for eight years for masterminding a cannabis-dealing ring.

Some good news came through as I was convalescing. Ian Sharples had received his release date from the Cyprus prison; he would be home just before Christmas 1992. I spent a few weeks taking it easy. My face was healing well but the slowest thing to recover was my left leg, where I had been stabbed in the thigh. Ian returned home to Blackpool quite subdued, though apart from looking a bit thinner he appeared in good health.

The annual Christmas Ball was being held at the famous Winter Gardens in Blackpool town centre. Ian, who had only been home a few days from his extended holiday in Cyprus, wanted to go but it didn't appeal to me. However, we were passing the Winter Gardens heading back to Promises after having a drink elsewhere in the town so Ian decided to go in to see his fiancée, Tracy Lowe. Tracy is a very good-looking girl, an ex-Miss Blackpool and a Miss Great Britain runner-up. No wonder he wanted to go in and meet up with her rather than stay with me. He had probably had a bit too much male-on-male company while he was in Cyprus.

I left Ian at the entrance to the Winter Gardens and returned to Promises, which is only a two-minute walk away. I had only been back in the club for five minutes when Ian walked through the side door, looking battered and bruised.

'What the fuck happened to you? I have only just left you two minutes ago.'

He went on to explain that the two doormen on duty at the Christmas Ball did not know him from Adam and had refused to let him in without a ticket. When Ian tried to explain his situation, one of the doormen, a cockney, had told him to fuck off or he would get it. Ian tried to appeal to their better nature and mentioned my name as being his pal, but through either not knowing or believing Ian or possibly not liking me, they both ended up jumping him.

I was very pissed off at hearing this; I knew Ian would not have started anything with the doormen because he had been very subdued since his return from Cyprus.

'Come on pal,' I said. 'Let's go and have a fucking word with them.'

As Ian and I approached the Winter Gardens, we noticed that the police armed response vehicle was parked outside the main doors. The two doormen were clearly visible just inside the doors.

'That's them,' said Ian, nodding in their direction.

Looking at the police van, I noticed it was my friend Martin Cooper, from the police social club incident (**see page xx**), and Nick Phillips who is married to a good friend of my wife Tanee and who I got on very well with.

Ian was looking a bit the worse for wear, so I said to him, 'You go back to Promises pal, while I go and see what is happening.'

Walking over to the police vehicle I was warmly greeted by my two friends. I was even passed a Christmas card from Nick and Julie to Tanee and myself. It was just a coincidence that the two officers were parked outside the Winter Gardens at that time, they had no knowledge of the earlier incident and I had no intention of telling them.

Shaking both of their hands and wishing them a happy Christmas, I headed for the Winter Gardens doors. I saw one of the doormen grimace when he recognised me and then he told his pal, who sneered in my direction. Turning my head back towards Martin and Nick, I said, 'You had better put your hats on lads, you are going to be busy in a minute.'

As I approached the two doormen, the larger of the two, the one that had sneered at me, said in a cockney accent, 'I don't give a fuck who you...'

That was as far as he got before I headbutted him. He

dropped like a dead pigeon falling from the sky, straight down. The other one jumped on my back to try to hold me but I threw him over my shoulder and clipped him with a right hand as he tried to get up. The next thing, I was being gripped by two policemen, neither of whom were wearing their hats, who both said at the same time, 'We thought you were joking, you mad bastard. What's going on?'

The cockney was knocked out cold and did not look like he was going to wake up at any time soon, so an ambulance had to be called. A police sergeant arrived on the scene and I was promptly arrested for suspicion of grievous bodily harm. As I was being led away in hand-cuffs, I thought to myself, this is fucking great, Sharpie's just come out of prison and it looks like I'm going in for Christmas. At least I would get to see Frank and Joe if I was banged up in the Preston nick.

I was waiting to be charged at the custody suite in Blackpool's main police station when Martin and Nick came into the room. They had a word with the custody sergeant who came over to me and said, 'Those two officers have told me that the doorman who is still at the Winter Gardens has refused to press charges and they seem to think that the doorman who is in hospital won't press charges either. So what I intend to do is put you into the holding cell out here.' He then asked me if I would agree to that, which of course I was only too happy to do. Sure enough a few hours later I was released without charge.

It turned out that the cockney doorman was new in town and was not impressed by names alone, even when the other lad had warned him. Still you must give him some credit, he stood his ground and took it like a man. It was just his behaviour and manner that let him down.

Ian soon got back into the swing of things and helped me with the running of the club. This soon brought him back out of his shell. Although thinking back, he never seemed too happy if any man winked at him from that time on. Ian went from strength to strength, opening the first floor of the premises as a nightclub and calling it the Cotton Club. The downstairs that had been Promises he gutted and turned into the Rose and Crown pub, which it still is today.

Ian then went on to buy an old warehouse next door that was in an alley next to the Scruffy Murphy's pub and fitted it out from scratch into a beautiful wine bar and restaurant. He called the place Mojo's and it was very successful until the horrible tax man took it all away.

Ian has moved out of Blackpool now. He lives in the country with his wife Tracy and his daughter Emily, my goddaughter, and they are all quite happy and successful.

17

Mr Magoo

I HAD BEEN pulled in again for questioning about a couple of alleged violent incidents where scumbags who owed people money had received a slap or two. The police had nothing concrete to go on but they wanted to talk to me about them anyway. What the heck, nothing different there.

I sat down with Ian and we gave it some thought, discussing where the business was going and things that had happened in the past involving the police. The way things were going, I was either going to end up dead, divorced or locked up. I came to the decision that I was going to sell my interest in the club to Ian and lie low for a bit. I thought this might remove me from the Lancashire Constabulary crosshairs for a while. I was fed up being a target for them bastards, they only had to get it right once and I was going down. I had to get it right every time and a person's luck can't keep lasting like that.

Tanee and I had decided to sell our house on Elizabeth Street and look for something a bit more upmarket. We ended up selling it for a very good profit so it was not long before we found a lovely detached bungalow right opposite Stanley Park. The price was not too high, especially for the area where the bungalow was, so we put in an offer and it was accepted. A date was arranged for us to take possession of our new home and we moved into the bungalow on the Thursday before Good Friday, 1993. I had some savings put by and so I decided to take a year off from finding a job and do any work that needed doing on the new house.

It was not long until I was getting bored and so I started to look for something to do. I was doing a bit of door work at the weekends but I wanted something more. I saw an advert in the local *Gazette* for bailiffs to collect unpaid magistrates' fines all across the country. It was the same as I had been doing for years – debt collecting – only this time it was legal. So I applied, and, astonishingly, ended up as a court-appointed bailiff.

I had to carry ID, which meant I had to behave myself on jobs because people could identify me, and I also had the right to call the police for back-up! Needless to say, I never did; that just didn't sit right with me. To tell the truth, though I worked as a bailiff for a while, I didn't like it. Some of the hard luck stories would make you weep. I went to collect from one guy only for him to tell me his wife had died and left him with four kids. I nearly paid what he owed myself.

I was also doing a bit of minding every now and then. One day I had travelled over to Liverpool from Blackpool with a local man who was involved in the music promotion industry. This man was carrying a large amount of cash in a holdall and had asked me to go with him to make sure it was not taken away from him by the wrong people. We arrived in a very rundown part of Toxteth, the scene of major riots in the early Eighties. A new Volkswagen Golf GTi pulled up close to where we were parked and the man with me got out of our car and walked over to the Golf. Ten minutes later he was back in the car with me and we were heading back to Blackpool.

'Steve,' the man said, 'did you see the bloke driving the Golf?'

I said yes, I had seen a youngish, light-skinned black

man wearing a shell suit.

'He is worth millions. In fact you would not believe how much he is worth.'

I thought to myself, bollocks. But his name was Curtis Warren. He was later to be jailed in Holland after a massive drugs operation for conspiring to smuggle heroin, cocaine, ecstasy and cannabis and was the subject of the best-seller *Cocky: The Rise and Fall of Curtis Warren, Britain's Biggest Drug Baron*.

As we pulled off the M55 motorway back in Blackpool, we were surrounded by police cars and forced to stop. The police tore the car apart looking for something. I think they thought I was taking the piss when I asked them what they were looking for, but they did not find anything and so they had to let us go on our way.

The man I was travelling with was later sentenced to nine years in prison for being involved in the supply of class A drugs. This is how it came about. A car travelling along one of our motorways was stopped by the police and during a search of the vehicle a very large amount of cash was found inside. The police arrested the driver when he could not explain where the money had come from or what it was for. The money was confiscated by the police until someone could come up with a satisfactory reason and physical evidence to claim it. So who was the person who came up with the required evidence and reclaimed all this cash, between £200,000 and £300,000? None other than Mark McGovern, better known in Blackpool as Magoo.

Now this made the police very unhappy, not only with Magoo but also the people that they suspected really owned the money. When this large amount was returned to Mark it was actually put into his lawyer's account. His lawyer at that time was a local man by the name of Steve Pope. Now Steve Pope liked to sail close to the wind himself (he is no longer a solicitor, but that is a different story). Unbeknown to Magoo, the police had put some kind of tracking order on this money and any time any of it was withdrawn or transferred they were to be informed immediately. I don't know what they expected to find in the car on the day they pulled us over, probably drugs, but as I mentioned earlier we had nothing in the car.

A long time later, on an early September morning, my youngest daughter Christie was due to start school at Stanley Infants. She was four at the time, so it was 1995. I awoke at six o'clock to what I thought was someone trying to knock down the house. I jumped from my bed and went into the hallway just as the front door caved in. It looked like an American SWAT team coming through the doorway. They didn't give me a chance to ask who they were there for (well, you never know). They had me face down and handcuffed before Tanee had woken up. I told you, that girl can sleep.

The officer in charge told me that I was under arrest for being involved in the supply of cocaine. Thank fuck for that. I had thought they were here for something else. I laughed at them and said, 'Fuck off, you know that's not my game.' When they had taken me away to the police station they tried to bring a drug sniffer dog that had been running around our garden into the house. Tanee, who was now wide awake and a bit pissed off, stopped them dead in their tracks and made them wipe the dog's paws. I love her.

The *Evening Gazette* ran the story the next day with the headlines saying, 'Millionaire Businessman Arrested, Drugs and Firearms Found.' What a load of bollocks. The firearm was a replica that Tanee had in her bedside drawer for when I was away from home; this was not illegal in the slightest. The drugs that were allegedly found were trace evidence that the dog had sniffed out on my work coat that I wore as a doorman. And to call me a millionaire was laughable.

I was taken to Blackpool Central police station and processed before being put into a cell. As I was walking past some occupied cells, I heard Magoo shouting, 'Who's that?'

I replied, 'It's me, Sinclair.'

I heard him say to himself, 'Fucking hell, what have they nicked him for, he'll kill me.'

It turned out that the police had had a suspected gang of drug dealers from Liverpool and Blackpool under surveillance for some time, in fact they had phone records going back eighteen months or more. This led to me being remanded for a short period before I was charged with being involved in the supply of class A drugs and other offences. The police alleged that I was a paid minder or muscle for this firm. My bank accounts and all assets were frozen whilst they were being investigated, not only mine but Tanee's as well. Any money paid into our accounts was accepted by the bank but no withdrawals or payments out were allowed, so all of our credit cards, standing orders and direct debits were blocked. It took Tanee a fair amount of time and effort to sort it all out but she did it and she never once blamed me for it. She knew that I would not be involved in supplying drugs.

The police and Crown Prosecution Service took it all the way, with us facing numerous appearances at Preston Crown Court. On what turned out to be the last occasion for some of us, our barristers were all called in for a discussion with the prosecution barristers. When they had finished talking with the other side, my barrister came back to me and said there was an offer on the table that Magoo was accepting. If he pleaded guilty to money laundering and being involved in the supply of Class A drugs, they were willing to let the charges against a man named Steven Wynn from Liverpool and myself be withdrawn and be left to lie on file. This would mean that Steven Wynn and I would walk away from the court that day as free men but if we were ever arrested on similar charges in the future they could bring up this case evidence to be used against us. Mark McGovern would then be sentenced as a guilty man as soon as reports from the Probation Service were completed. Fair play to Magoo, he accepted their deal there and then. He received nine years but he still never learned a lesson from it. Once he got out of prison, after serving five or six years, he went straight back into the same game and the last I heard was once more awaiting sentencing on similar charges.

During the long and dark period of my bank accounts and credit and debit cards being frozen, Frank Bruno was due to fight Mike Tyson again after nearly nailing him in their first fight for the world heavyweight title. The contest was to take place at the MGM Hotel in Las Vegas and quite a few good friends of mine from Blackpool fancied going over to America to watch it. A good pal of mine named Steve Barratt, a building contractor who is worth a few quid, knew about the predicament I was in and offered to pay for my flight, accommodation and a fight ticket. All I would need was some spending money.

A couple of grand would be enough, seeing as how I am not a gambler. Where could I get that from? Debt collecting or 'taxing', either would probably suffice. Well, the money was soon sorted and in my pocket. How I got it, that's another story.

We arrived at Las Vegas on the Tuesday with the fight taking place on the Saturday. We were booked in at the Camelot Hotel which is opposite the MGM so that was quite handy. I was sharing a room with Glen Walsh. Glen, who is the son of Michael 'Mixie' Walsh, is a lovely bloke and just as game as his dad.

By the time we were allowed into our rooms everybody was knackered. It was four o'clock in the afternoon and we had all been drinking on the plane on the way over. Most of the group decided to have a rest before meeting up later on that evening.

When Glen got undressed for bed I was gobsmacked. He was wearing a thong. I had never seen a man in a thong before. Big Dave Garside was in the next room to us so I called him in to have a look. This started to get Glen a bit paranoid, especially when we both started to say what a 'nice ass' he had. Glen wrapped himself up in his sheet like a cocoon, leaving just his face uncovered.

'You can't get me now,' he said, quite seriously.

'Oh no?' I said, unzipping my flies. 'What about that lovely mouth?'

I was in tears of laughter watching him try to get out of the safe cocoon that he had wrapped himself so securely in.

When we woke up it was close to midnight. Where the fuck was everyone?

After a quick shower (separate), we went down to the casino for something to eat. A few drinks later, Glen was telling me about his aunt and uncle, who lived in Tucson, Arizona. His uncle Jack was a big American cowboy type who I had met once when he had visited Blackpool. After a few more drinks, we found ourselves at McCarran Airport getting on a plane to Phoenix, without telling any of our friends. Once we got to Phoenix we tried to hire a car but my credit cards were frozen and Glen did not have any, so we ended up at rent-a-wreck where they would accept cash. We were given a huge Oldsmobile that had seen better days but what the hell, we were on an adventure. With no worries in the world, we got into our rent-a-wreck and headed in the general direction of Tucson.

About one hour into the journey it started to rain quite heavily. The window wipers didn't work; so we stopped and took one of them off and carried on with the window open, using the wiper manually. When we finally found Glen's uncle's house, he answered the door with, 'Hello Steve, what are you doing here?' as if it was the most normal thing in the world, which blew our minds. They made us very welcome.

Jack said that we could go shooting if we fancied it and opened what I thought was a cupboard. Fuck me, there were more guns in that room than in the firing range the last time I had visited Las Vegas. The next day we spent hours at an outdoors shooting club, firing hundreds of rounds from different types of guns. We also took a day trip into Nogales, Mexico, where we were inundated with offers of very cheap cocaine and other illegal items.

The last night that we were staying at Jack's, Glen went out with his cousin for a barbecue up a mountain somewhere. I was taking it easy and so I stayed in. The next morning, I was up bright and early and was watching the local news with Jack. The main headline was about a local monument of great historical interest burning down on this mountain. Fire teams from all surrounding areas were tackling this blaze. Just then the door opened and Glen and his cousin came in, covered in soot and looking very sheepish. *Oops.*

When we finally got back to Las Vegas, Bruno lost to Tyson, but I don't think anyone expected anything different. Glen visited his first lap dancing club and fell in love, not with one of the gorgeous naked girls that drape themselves over you but with the idea of opening a similar club in Blackpool. Anyone who has watched the Sky Television series on lap dancing clubs in Blackpool will recognise Glen and his wife Charlie as the owners of Sinless, a top class establishment.

The Adam and Eve nightclub that Ian Sharples had owned was bought by Andrew Trotter. Andy, who came from Sheffield, turned out to be related to a good friend of mine. At the time I was looking after a club on Topping Street, called High Society, with my pal Steve Daley.

On the opening night for the Adam and Eve – probably under the tenth new owner since the club had been going – my wife and I went in with some friends. I was introduced to Andy, who said he had been hearing stories about Blackpool and me in particular for a long time. Andy, who is six or seven years younger than me, is an ex-Sheffield Wednesday football hooligan with a tattoo saying 'Made in Sheffield' on the back of his neck. He has plenty of contacts in that game so we ended up getting on really well together. He had moved to Blackpool with his wife Julie and his youngest son Benjamin and over the following months our friendship developed.

One night I was at the High Society club with Steve Daley when a local lad came in and told us that there was loads of trouble down at the Adam and Eve club with football fans. Our venue was pretty quiet at that time so I jumped into a taxi and got down there as quickly as I could. Arriving at the club, I could see a number of police officers separating a large group of men across the road from another large group of men that was outside the Adam and Eve. I walked straight through the group outside the club and went in the front door. Inside the club were even more men.

Finally I found Andy and asked him if he was okay. He laughed and said, 'Yes, these are my pals from Sheffield. Those other cunts were Wolves fans.'

After he had introduced me to some of the Sheffield firm – big Weenie, Flynnie, Paddy and Eddie, to name a few, all good solid lads – I saw what could only be described as a confused look come over Andrew's face.

'Hang on a minute, you have come all the way from High Society by yourself and just walked straight through this firm to make sure that I am all right?' He thought a bit longer, then he said, 'My doormen have just shit themselves and got out of the way. Fuck it! Why don't you come and work here for me?'

Andrew had a business partner who was also from Sheffield. This individual had a hotel in Blackpool and it was he who had wanted Steve Hill's firm on the door. Andy said, 'They can stay but I still want Sinclair here.' The long and short of it was that Steve Hill turned up with Tommy Salt and some other lads. They listened to what Andy's partner said and then to Andy. Steve Hill then said no, his men could not work with me. He obviously believed all the bullshit about me being involved in organised crime.

So in the end Andy's partner lost the money that he had put into the business, Steve Hill lost the door and also lost the doormen because they quit his company to work with me. My show of friendship had earned me a true friend who stood by his word and gave me the job.

I was away on holiday one week and Andy was driving my car, a black Audi Quattro with A5 GBH as a licence plate, when the police pulled him over for some reason and searched the car. They found a gun-cleaning kit in the boot but no weapons or firearms. Getting a search warrant, the police proceeded to turn over Andy's house. They couldn't do mine because I was not in charge of the vehicle plus I was out of the country. One of the CID officers told Andy that they had done a full PNC (Police National Computer check) and although he was a face in Sheffield he had moved up to the first division with the people he was associating with now. If that is true, all I can say is that he was ready to move up.

One evening, after the club had closed, Andy and I went to the infamous Shalimar Gardens, an Indian restaurant in Talbot Square, for some supper. The owner then was an Indian named Dave. Now I had plenty of history with Dave from the Promises days, when we used to go there all the time, and I had been arrested there for GBH and wounding charges a couple of times. As we were sat ordering our meal, I looked around the restaurant, as you do. There were a few local customers that I knew and plenty of others that I didn't.

Dave came across to our table and asked if he could

have a word. He pointed out two men sat at a table on the far side of the room. One was black and one was white but both had something in common: they had huge muscles.

'They are refusing to pay their bill,' said Dave with a worried expression. 'Can you have a word with them, please?'

I was winding down after work and I had just started to relax. Typical. As I stood up to walk over to their table, both men also stood up preparing to leave. The black man was about my height but about three stone heavier, the white man was about four or five inches taller than me and about three stone heavier. I must admit I actually thought about paying their bill for them and asking them if they had enjoyed their evening.

Dave put a stop to that by saying something like, 'You will have to pay your bill now,' and pointing to me. I could see them weighing me up and not being overly impressed with what they saw. The black guy fronted me up and smirked.

'Why, who is going to make us?' he said.

I glanced to my right and saw Andy facing the white guy and thought, at least I will have someone to talk to in the hospital. I cannot tell a lie, my arse was twitching, but as I have said before, when I'm scared I am more dangerous because I won't back down. I looked at the size of the big black smirking head right in front of me and thought to myself, I can't miss that fucking thing. With that thought still in my mind, I smashed my right elbow into his chin quicker than some people could blink their eyes. He dropped like he had been shot.

Guess what my newly-promoted-to-the-first-division mate did? He looked that huge white guy right in the eye and said, 'Do you want him to do that to you? If not, pay your fucking bill!'

The man looked at his pal who was still unconscious on the floor at my feet, then pulled his wallet out from his back pocket and asked, 'Will plastic be okay?'

He's smarter than he looks is our Andy.

Things didn't work out too well for Andy at the Adam and Eve club so he sold it and bought a boozer in the North Shore area called the Mount Pleasant. Unpleasant more like, the area is surrounded by bedsits and DHSS hotels and as such was inundated with drug addicts and scumbags. After a few weeks we had cleaned the pub out of all the undesirables and the word had spread that they and their kind were not welcome anymore. Nice people started to use the pub again, people like the Glaister family, Bill and Joan and their sons Steve and John. Steve and John were doormen in the town and we all became good friends; sadly Steve died a few years ago, gone but not forgotten by his family and friends.

Andy had also purchased the lease on another pub in South Shore called Legends, so this was keeping us busy too. At the same time, I had made the acquaintance of some of Scotland's most notorious gangsters.

18

The Glasgow Connection

AS IF THERE weren't enough Scotsmen in Blackpool already. My sister Lorraine was having a drink or two in the Stix nightclub, which was part of the Blackpool dog racing track, when she was approached by a dark-eyed Scotsman of small stature. The man was extremely polite which impressed my sister greatly.

'Excuse me miss, I am very sorry to bother you but someone has just pointed you out to me and told me that you are Steve Sinclair's sister,' he said. 'A very good friend of mine once said to me that if I ever found myself in Blackpool that I should look Steve up and mention my friend's name.'

After Lorraine had chatted to this charming Scotsman for a few minutes, she asked his name.

'Billy,' he replied. 'Billy Ferris from Glasgow.'

Billy is the older brother of Paul Ferris, the infamous Glasgow enforcer and gangster. Although our Lorraine was infatuated with the wee charmer, Billy was in fact a convicted murderer who had escaped from custody and was in Blackpool on the run from the police.

I must admit that I took to Billy myself, as did my mum and dad. In the end any help Billy might have thought about asking me for was not needed, seeing as how my sister had fallen in love with him and moved him into her house on Kensington Road.

Billy kept coming up with certain business schemes that he would try to get me involved in but I had promised Tanee that I wouldn't do anything with him. Every couple of days a few lads from Glasgow carrying shooters would turn up at our Lorraine's house with a parcel of money or a parcel of something else.

One night, as I was working on the door of the High Society club along with my pal Steve Daley, a taxi pulled up outside. The door opened and two men in suits climbed out. The first one looked liked an accountant and the second one like a bank manager. I thought I would be better letting them know that the club was full of young tossers before they let their taxi leave.

Stepping down a step, I said, 'Excuse me gents, I don't think this club will suit you.'

The accountant looked at me and in a pleasant Scottish accent said, 'Hi, we are looking for Steve Sinclair.'

I looked the pair of them over. They definitely weren't the Old Bill and they didn't seem to be much of a threat.

'I'm Steve Sinclair. What can I do for you?'

The accountant put his hand out to shake mine. 'I'm Paul Ferris and this is Rab Carruthers. I believe you know my brother Billy.'

Paul Ferris was a notorious Glasgow hit man and enforcer. Rab Carruthers, an older version of Paul, had moved away from Glasgow and had been living in Manchester for some years running his own organised crime firm. I was going to have to get my threat radar seen too. I wouldn't say that we became good friends but we did become good acquaintances, in fact we nearly became family.

One evening we were having a drink in a pub in Blackpool when Paul asked me what I carried. When I asked him what he meant, he showed me a nine-millimetre semi-automatic nestled beneath his jacket in a shoulder holster. I explained to him that in Blackpool during the season the number of fights I could be involved in in just one night made it impossible for me to carry a gun. I asked him how he managed.

Being quite serious, he looked me directly in the eye and stated, 'Steve, I don't fight mate. If they come for me they either get shot or stabbed.'

Paul would come to Blackpool quite often and stay at the Verona Hotel, run by our cockney pal Paul Jonas, and every now and then a few of us would travel up the road to be Paul's guests in Glasgow. On one such trip, Andy Trotter and I went up. Paul had arranged a room for us in the Moat House Hotel. We had a lovely meal and then spent the evening in a club called Victoria's. We were treated like royalty.

We had driven up from Blackpool in a brand new Shogun 4x4, which we left overnight in the hotel car park. As soon as we set off on our return journey, we knew that there was something different about the vehicle. It had been a very quiet car on the journey up but on the way back we could hear wind gusting through the seal of the windscreen. We checked the vehicle thoroughly but didn't find anything missing, or planted for that matter. It was only some time later that someone told us that a favourite trick of the security services was to take out the windscreen of a vehicle and use specialist bugging equipment that could pick up any conversation inside. Andy was quite relieved when the Shogun was nicked and burnt out by joyriders.

We had quite a few acquaintances in common and although we never did business together we did do each other a favour or two. Billy Ferris was in Blackpool for quite some time and although he was supposed to be keeping a low profile he did manage to put himself about. He and my sister Lorraine got engaged to be married but before anything could happen Billy was arrested in Blackpool and returned to Barlinnie Prison in Glasgow. Lorraine was tried and convicted for harbouring an escaped convict. She continued to visit Billy, who was now in the prison up in Perth, but their relationship was doomed.

Lorraine then met and married a Blackpool man named Mark Singleton, who was originally from Australia. She moved to Australia and now lives just outside Brisbane. She and her family were part of the television show *A New Life Down Under*. She has since split up with her husband but she is very happy there. I have visited them a couple of times and loved it. If my wife was willing I would gladly sell up here and move out there but sadly she isn't.

Billy was finally released from prison but regrettably he went on to kill again and is now back inside. Paul was arrested for firearms offences when he was caught out in a sting operation involving the police and the British Security Service, MI5. He was caught with about ten machine guns and was sent to prison for ten years. He has recently been released and has become a successful author in his own right and is having his story, *Vendetta*, made into a film.

Good luck Paul and I send my best wishes to Billy.

I was well off my own manor; doing a favour for a friend. The idea was that my face was not known. I was a complete stranger even to people passing by. I could walk in and deliver the message and then walk away without being seen again. Hopefully. A lot of villains are arrested because of passers-by recognising them even though the villain would not recognise the witness if he was face to face with them.

I was carrying a sawn-off, double-barrelled, twelve-bore shotgun with a customised grip. I preferred a shotgun to a handgun in these situations, there are so many replica handguns about now that some people wouldn't think twice about having a go, but with a sawn-off the effect is different. The two barrels seem to grow in size when you are looking down the wrong end of them and if you look up from the shotgun into a pair of eyes that are showing no feelings or emotion, it can be quite daunting.

The man I was there to see was trying to avoid paying a rather large amount of money to my friend. I was going to try to convince him to pay up before it escalated any further. His premises were on an industrial estate a couple miles from the city centre. An appointment had been made for me to see him under an assumed name and business venture to ensure that he was on site. I was suited and booted and carrying a briefcase and had a local man driving for me. I was under no illusions about this being a walk in the park. The man was a known player and I did not expect him to pay up without some form of resistance. The appointment had been made at a time when most of the workforce would not be present, to minimise the risk of anyone else getting involved. I did not want to face some have-a-go hero.

Everything was going exactly to plan. I should have known it would fuck up somewhere along the way.

I entered the office, taking care to make sure I knew my way out. As I say, this guy was a bit of a player and I was very aware that I was by myself. There were boxing photos and trophies scattered around the room, pictures of Jim Watt and the man opposite me cuddling each other.

Fuck it. There was no one else there, so I decided to get it over with. I opened the briefcase and removed the sawn-off shotgun. Pointing the business end at him, I said, 'I have a message for you from one of your associates. Stop fucking about and pay up or the next time you get a visit, you will get it in both legs.'

Turning slightly, I fired one barrel into the boxing photos just to let him know the threat was real. The glass, photos and frames were shattered.

I looked him straight in the eye. He hadn't moved a muscle. *Sorted*, I thought to myself. *Time to fuck off quick*.

Picking up the briefcase, I turned towards the door. I had started to place the shotgun inside the case when I felt a searing pain across my left wrist, followed by the sound of a gunshot. *Fuck!* The cunt was shooting at me from a distance of twelve feet.

My left hand had opened in a spasm, causing me to drop the briefcase, but I still had hold of the shotgun in my right hand. Jumping backwards, I twisted to face the desk. The man who had just shot me was looking at me in horror while trying to clear a jammed cartridge from his automatic pistol. No wonder I like revolvers so much. Thank you God!

Seeing me swing the shotgun up in his direction, the cunt dropped behind his desk. I didn't know how experienced he was with firearms or clearing a jammed pistol but I knew that I had only one shot left and that I had to get out of there as quickly as I could. I saw that there was a gap between the tiled floor and the bottom of the desk. Lowering my aim, I fired at the tiled floor beneath the desk. I knew that a good percentage of the shotgun pellets would ricochet up from the floor and cause some injury. I heard a scream and the sound of his gun hitting the floor. That was good enough for me. I was out of there.

My friend was paid the outstanding debt as soon as the injured player came out of hospital. He had not been too badly hurt but like me he would carry some scars to remind him of our meeting. I was very lucky; the bullet skimmed my wrist, just missing my Rolex. I would have been really pissed off if it had smashed my favourite watch. I ended up with a two-inch scar across the top of my left wrist that reminds me of how very lucky I was that day.

I finally gave up debt collecting when a man that I'd

had a quiet word with in Blackpool killed himself. I had been approached by a friend of mine named Billy, who owns a large double glazing window company. A builder owed him a substantial amount and didn't seem too keen on paying him back. Billy was going away for a couple of weeks on holiday and informed me that there was some work that this builder could do for him that would cancel the outstanding debt. If this was done, Billy would then pay me a percentage to cover my fee.

I had the builder's address and description. The man was big and shaggy and liked big motorbikes. That was all I needed, a big biker type. Still you have to take the rough with the smooth. I found the guy one early evening at his home in Blackpool and I explained things to him. The next morning I received a phone call from a friend of mine who was a doorman at a town centre pub. The conversation went something like this.

'Hi Steve, it's Mick. Don't take this the wrong way but have you been to see so-and-so about a debt?'

'Yes. Why?'

'Well he came in here last night because he has been seeing the landlady since he split up with his wife. He asked some questions about you, saying that you were on his case now. Anyway, he went home and hung himself.'

I said, 'You're joking, aren't you?'

'No.'

I thought to myself there and then, enough is enough.

When my pal Billy returned from sunning himself he contacted me to see what if anything had happened. I asked him if he wanted the good news or the bad news.

'The bad news first,' he said, with a worried look on his face.

'I talked to your man about the money he owed you and advised him on some of the options that were available to him. He decided on one that I didn't offer and now there is no chance of getting the money. He's dead.'

Billy almost fainted. 'What's the fucking good news?' he sobbed.

'I didn't kill him and do you want to buy a motorbike?'

When I think back over the years about some of the debts I have recovered or tried to recover, we have taken cars, motorbikes, caravans, jewellery, fingers and ears and, of course, money. Nowadays I don't take any debt collecting jobs, but I still know plenty of people who will.

19

Get the Ginger-headed One

PETER 'THE GINGER-HEADED One' McCarthy, a pal of mine from Promises days who could start a fight in an empty room, applied to a local pub company for a job as a public house manager. He got the job and they gave him a beautiful pub. The only problem was that it was smack bang in the middle of Salford.

Peter and his fiancée at the time, a young lady by the name of Dawn, settled in at the Adelphi Riverside pub, situated on the bank of the river near to Salford University.

The place was lovely, but at that time there was a lot of trouble with criminal gangs after protection money. Roger Cook of *The Cook Report* did a special on Salford and the problems the area was facing with protection rackets. Landlords were being offered protection for their premises and, if they refused, fights would break out and the place or the landlord would get smashed. The landlord would then get the offer again. If he or she refused once more or contacted the police, the pub would suffer an arson attack and would end up as a burnt-out wreck. Driving around Salford it looked like a derelict area, with fire-damaged pubs everywhere. The police said on *The Cook Report* that if they could find a landlord willing to stand up against this gang, they could take action against them.

On a sunny Sunday afternoon, Andy Trotter and I decided to drive through to Salford to see Peter as it was his birthday. When we arrived the pub was full of customers. Peter came out of the kitchen after being told by one of his bar staff that we had arrived. On seeing him my first thought was that he had been in a car accident, but it turned out that he had received a beating the night before from a gang of lads claiming to be from Paul Massey's firm.

I had known Peter from when I was at Just Ji's. He was the doorman at the Station pub across the road who I had helped out one night when he was being attacked. Peter later came to work for me as my assistant at Promises when Ian Sharples, Frank Tonner and Joe Sweeney were all banged up in jail. Whenever a big fight broke out that we all had to get involved in, I would always shout out, 'Get the ginger-headed one,' to no-one in particular. This referred to Peter's ginger hair and it worked quite well a few times, with people from both sides throwing punches at him. I would always have a grin on my face after any such incident; a lot of people thought it was because I enjoyed a fight but in reality I was smiling at Pete. When he finally found out, he didn't see the funny side of this for some time.

Paul Massey ran a big gang and was alleged to control certain rackets in the Salford area and further afield. At the time, he was banged up in Strangeways Prison on remand for an attempted murder charge. A documentary film-making crew were following Paul around and during a fight outside a nightclub he allegedly stabbed someone. He was eventually jailed for ten years for wounding with intent. Now we all know that business carries on as usual when the main man is in jail, but there is also the potential for other people to use his name or to try muscling in on his territory. So whether this gang really was his firm or just some chancers putting his name forward to scare people, I don't know. But that's who they made out they were.

Later in the day we were joined by Steven Heap, Peter's cousin. Steve was a big man and had worked the doors in Blackpool himself. He was now running a pub in Eccles, just a few miles down the road. I had met him a few times and liked him. He had a good, solid reputation in the Blackpool area.

As the afternoon moved into the evening, the pub was still quite busy. Andy, Steve and I were sat talking to some nice people we had just met when a team of lads, about twelve strong, came walking into the pub. To say they looked out of place would be an understatement. I could only describe them as toerags who thought they were the boys. They were glaring at the customers nearest to them and jostling people out of their way.

As Peter came from the office, he saw this team of lads and his face went white. He turned quickly and disappeared back the way he had come. I had been seen taking an interest by one of the gang and, as Peter disappeared, I stood up and started walking towards them to find out what was happening with my pal. Obviously I had half an idea who they were, but they didn't have a clue who I was.

The individual who had seen me moving spoke to the one I suspect was their leader. He looked at me and stepped forward. 'What the fuck do you want?' he growled.

I just punched him on the chin and kept on walking forward as he fell to the ground. The biggest one of the toerags, who had tattoos on his neck and hands and a shaven head, took out his false teeth and rushed at me. I blocked a wild punch from him with my left arm, grabbed his throat with my right hand and lifted and twisted at the same time. His own momentum caused his legs to leave the ground and travel upwards to my waist height. I then slammed him down, back first, onto the floor.

Andy Trotter and Steve Heap were right behind me

and they took the brunt of the first charge from the rest of the gang. I don't really know why but I just focused all my attention on this cunt I had hold of. I was squeezing his throat with my right hand whilst looking directly into his eyes. Certain throat holds can cause a certain amount of paralysis in the human body and apparently I was using one at that time. I saw the bravado vanish and the fear appear as he realised he was helpless. Then the fear turned into panic as he found he could no longer breathe properly.

'I can't breathe,' he gasped. 'I can't breathe.'

I bent lower so he could hear me and said, 'Don't you think I know that, you cunt. I am the last thing you are ever going to see.' I carried on squeezing.

The next thing I remember was hearing Pete's voice saying, 'Steve, it's over, you can let him go now.'

I didn't really want to but I looked up to see what was happening. Sure enough, all the toerags had been battered and were corralled into the locked conservatory that faced the river. I still didn't want to let go but I did in the end. Pete turned to the cowering team and told them to 'pick up your friend and fuck off'.

It turned out that after the first charge, Andy and Steve Heap had been pushed backwards past the point where I had hold of this geezer. The toe rags had swarmed all over me trying to get me off of their pal, but I didn't notice. Andy picked up a stool and started laying into them. Steve was also moving forward again. Then Peter came back from his office where he had been to collect his baseball bat. Now Pete isn't shy about using weapons and his attack coming from the rear completely broke them. The pub had apparently emptied at the start of the trouble.

As we were having a medicinal brandy, Steve Heap showed us one of his thumbs. It had very nearly been bitten through. I was also starting to feel some pain; the back of my head was one big lump where I had been repeatedly hit. Lifting my sweatshirt revealed numerous bite marks and boot prints. Steve Heap would have to go to the hospital with his thumb, it was in a proper mess.

I asked Peter how much damage he thought he had done with his bat.

He replied, 'A fair bit, I got some good hits in, why?'

'Because there is a good chance that some of them will be there.'

I borrowed a straight razor from Pete and headed to the hospital with Andy and Steve. We left Pete looking after his pub in a sulk because he couldn't come with us. On arrival at Hope Hospital, we entered the accident and emergency department. We immediately saw the group of men that had been at the Adelphi Riverside.

We booked Steve in at the triage desk for treatment. Steve tried to say it was a dog bite but they could tell the difference. Then Andy and I went to have a quick follow-up with the lads. They were so busy talking among themselves that they didn't notice us approach. They were sat by the gents' toilets and so they were used to men going past them and into the toilet. It was only when we actually stopped and stood right in front of them that they looked up at us.

It was like something from a cartoon; all their jaws dropped at the same time and their eyes nearly popped out of their heads. Not one of them moved. Looking at their faces I could not see my pal with the tattoos or the kid I suspected was their main boy. When I asked them where he was, one of them lifted his arm and pointed at a soundproofed telephone booth across the room.

Nice one, son.

They still didn't move as we turned and headed over to the phone booth. I took up a position directly behind the man on the phone. He was talking to someone about what had happened earlier, so I just waited patiently. It took a few seconds for him to realise that someone was stood right behind him. Glancing quickly round, he registered my face and must have thought of me as someone he knew because he smiled at me and carried on talking.

Less than a second later, his brain must have placed me in the right compartment because he just dropped the telephone and started to scream for help. I had reached into my back pocket for the cutthroat razor and was bringing it up with the full intention of slitting his nose right down the middle.

Andy grabbed my arm and said, 'Steve, it's the Old Bill.'

Looking over his shoulder, I saw that two traffic police had entered A&E. Looking back at my intended victim, I smiled and said, 'Lucky boy.' With that, we turned and walked away.

Returning to the Adelphi pub after Steve Heap had been treated, we sat up most of the night waiting to see if we would get a surprise visit. We were woken by a couple of officers from Salford CID banging on the door. When they interviewed Peter about the previous night's entertainment, they asked him if a Mr Sinclair from Blackpool was still here. Peter looked suitably shocked until they explained that they had PNC'd the registrations of the cars in the car park and the black Audi with the A5 GBH number had come up with my name and address.

They told us that they did not want a war breaking out between Salford and Blackpool. They had already contacted the Blackpool police once they had PNC'd my car registration and been given my history. I explained to them that we were just in the right place at the right time as far as Pete was concerned and that we had no intention of starting anything.

It turned out that there was a police informer within the gang of men from the night before and that he had phoned the police and told them that the gang were planning to kill the landlord in retaliation for what had happened. Peter was moved out of the Adelphi Riverside by his company, who put a new landlord into the pub and changed it into a students bar named the Old Pint Pot. Some time later I heard that this landlord had agreed to pay the going rate as requested by these gangs. This worked out at £50 a week. Unbelievable.

Peter and his cousin Steve ended up buying a leasehold public house named the Cross Keys in the Shropshire town of Oswestry. The pub was very successful for some time but the majority of the locals weren't too keen on Peter. He ended up doing some time in prison for wounding with intent; he bit a man's top lip off after the man had hit Peter over the head with a bottle.

Steve kept the business running well whilst Pete was away and when he was released from jail I went and picked him up and took him back to Oswestry. Pete and Steve also bought the lease on another building in the same town and turned it into another pub that they called DT's. This was after his daughter, Devon Taylor, though of course you get the DT's when you drink too much. They had a good local man by the name of Wayne looking after the security for them. It would have been a full time job knowing how Pete was with the locals.

Some of us Blackpool lads used to travel over on a Saturday for a laugh. We used to get on okay with the locals, there was a big travellers community there and as you can guess those boys will always find a fight especially at the weekend. I ended up getting on very well with them, so Peter and Steve asked me if I would be willing to travel over on the weekends to help them.

I worked over in Oswestry for about twelve months, helping them to look after the two pubs, the Cross Keys and DT's. Some people got the wrong idea and thought I was there as Peter's minder. This led to a few misunderstandings where a couple of people ended up getting a slap when there was no real need.

As it turned out, I also ended up having to give Pete a

slap when he lost the plot. This made most of the town very happy, in fact a police patrol car stopped as Peter was on the floor outside of the Cross Keys pub and I was stood over him. When they realised it was Peter McCarthy on the deck, they actually smiled at me and then drove away.

Peter started dating a young lady by the name of Susan Rees-Jones. Susan was the estranged wife of Trevor Rees-Jones. If you are wondering where you have heard that name, Trevor was Princess Diana's bodyguard and the only survivor of the car crash in Paris that killed Dodi Al Fayed and Diana. Trevor and Sue are both from Oswestry; as you can guess this led to a certain amount of tension from some people in the area, but none from Trevor, who was always a gentleman. That man has my utmost respect, top man.

I was working at Oswestry as I reached my fortieth birthday. Tanee bought me a return ticket to Bangkok for my present – what a girl. I went over with Ian Sharples, Andy Trotter and Dougie Isles, who was married to a Thai girl from the Chang Mai area in the northern provinces of Thailand. I can't really write anything about it because we all agreed with each other, 'What happens in Thailand stays in Thailand.' But needless to say we all had a great time. For my fiftieth birthday I have told Tanee that she can buy me a single ticket!

My daughter Kelly gave me the news that I was going to be a granddad. There's a birthday present that will last a long time.

Peter and Steven ended up falling foul of the licensing sergeant for that area. It all happened on one Saturday night in the summer, when Peter and Steve were both off duty and at a family do. The licensing sergeant came into DT's and started playing up. It turned out that they had let the licence lapse. Anyway the sergeant had two large constables with him. Both were in shirt-sleeve order because the weather was so nice but both of them were wearing leather gloves. This got my back up straight away and I ended up asking them politely, well not that politely, to leave the premises, which they did because the offence that was being committed was not an arrestable offence.

Later that night, after talking with Steven Heap about the incident, I decided to phone the local police station and apologise to the sergeant, because I hadn't been that polite earlier. When I finally got through to him he told me to 'piss off' and said that I would be receiving a summons.

On the Sunday morning, July 4, 1998, I received a phone call from my brother Colin to tell me that our father had died. I was heartbroken; I really loved my dad.

The drive that morning through from Oswestry to Blackpool was the worst of my life. I must have got back to Blackpool on remote control, I was that gutted.

My dad, Joe, had been poorly for some time and I had last seen him on the Thursday afternoon at the Blackpool Victoria Hospital, when he had just been admitted as a patient. Luckily my last words to him had been, 'I love you Dad, see you after the weekend.' I gave him the thumbs-up and left to make my way to Oswestry. So at least I had no issues to contend with.

For the next two years, every time I left my mother I made sure that I told her I loved her, because I knew soon that it would be the last time. My mother passed away on July 13 in the year 2000 and I still miss them both every day of my life.

Pete and Steve ended up losing the pubs but that didn't stop me receiving a summons alleging that I had sold alcohol without a licence. During the court session, the licensing sergeant was very smug giving his evidence until my brief asked him about a certain phone call that I had made that same night. At first he claimed he had not heard from me but the phone logs showed that he had received a call from the Cross Keys. When he recalled the conversation, my brief, Tim Mitchell, asked him what notes had he made regarding this call. When he admitted that he had not made any notes or record of our conversation, my solicitor asked for the case against me to be dismissed, which it was. Result!

Peter McCarthy went on to marry Sue and have a baby boy. They then went on to get a divorce and Pete ended up living in Thailand and has since married a Thai girl and had another baby, a boy again. He now lives on one of the small islands near Koh Samui and is a Paddi master diving instructor. We continue to have some laughs together especially out there in Thailand. And yes, what happens in Thailand stays in Thailand.

Fuck me. They were back again, with their balaclavas on, knocking on the front door with a sledgehammer. What the fuck is wrong with the doorbell?

'Stephen Sinclair you are under arrest.' Blah, blah, blah.

I was charged with wounding with intent and conspiracy. I was in Crown Court again, this time accused of being a hitman for hire. The police classed this as a major incident because a serving Blackpool officer was involved and as such the case was to be moved out of the town, to Burnley Crown Court. The Crown Prosecution Service, on the advice of the Regional Crime Squad, had put an Iranian man and another witness into the witness protection programme and by all accounts had set them up with a kebab shop in Nottingham.

When I had to attend an identification parade, it was held at the Longsight police station in Manchester. I turned up at the police station to see a police helicopter hovering over-head and armed officers outside. My friend Andy Trotter, who accompanied me, later told me that he was watched the whole time I was inside the station.

The Iranian man and the other witness both identified me, which didn't surprise me that much as they both knew me. The story told to the court was that this Iranian had worked as a waiter at an Indian restaurant in the centre of Blackpool, but had quit after falling out with the owner. Later he saw the restaurateur's girlfriend – who happened to be a serving Blackpool police officer – in a nightclub and insulted her. The couple then allegedly paid me to sort out the Iranian guy. The police accused me of entering his home and beating him to within an inch of his life. They produced a brass knuckleduster that they had found at my home as evidence and they also claimed that I had beaten him with a household iron.

The WPC and her boyfriend were also charged with inflicting GBH with intent in what the prosecution called a 'contract beating'. A Regional Crime Squad officer stood in the dock at the court and stated to the jury, 'Stephen Sinclair is a very dangerous man and we believe he would have little or no compunction about killing someone.' I had to ask what 'compunction' meant; it means scruples or guilt. What a cheeky twat.

On the last morning of a trial that had lasted for over two weeks, I turned up with Ian Sharples, Andy Trotter and another lad, to see the Indian restaurant owner and the policewoman both carrying bags.

'What are they for?' I asked naively.

They both looked at me and said that their barristers had told them that they were very likely going to prison for five years each. I replied that my barrister had not said anything like that to me.

The next thing we knew, the prosecution were offering us a deal if we accepted actual bodily harm. Blah, blah, blah. The policewoman approached me and told me that her boyfriend was willing to accept the deal, but she wanted to know what I was going to do. I smiled and said, 'I'm not guilty, why would I accept a deal that makes me guilty and sends me to prison?'

She smiled back at me and then turned away and told her barrister, 'No deal.'

The presiding judge, His Honour Judge Duckworth, whom I had been in front of before on different charges, when summing up the case described me to the jury as *man au natural* – 'A man that, if you were in trouble, you would be very pleased to have on your side.' He then went on to tell the jury, 'But you have also heard the detective from the Regional Crime Squad inform you of their beliefs concerning Mr Sinclair ...'

The jury went out just before lunch. The outcome was uncertain; the prosecution had made a pretty good case against us. We were still allowed to leave the court building, so my friends took me across the road to a pub. I had a few pints and a couple of vitamin E's just in case. I thought, bollocks, if I'm getting sent down I don't want those bastards from the Regional Crime Squad to gloat if I start getting upset. I had also passed all my jewellery over to Ian just in case the worst happened.

Not long after we had returned to the court, the jury came back with their decision. Sitting in the dock waiting for the verdict to be announced, I couldn't stop smiling to myself. I'm sure the judge and the police must have thought I had fixed the jury when the verdict came back NOT GUILTY but I hadn't, I was just off my head.

The nickname Teflon started to be used about me quite a bit, but I said, 'Not guilty means not guilty, not what a lucky bastard you are.' The party continued for the next couple of days at the Mount Pleasant pub.

Those days at the Mount Pleasant pub in North Shore and the Legends pub in South Shore were good times. There was a team of us that worked the two pubs, mostly lads, as these weren't the type of pubs that you could have young ladies working in by themselves.

On a very hot Saturday we had a sign outside the pub saying 'Topless Bar Staff'. A large group of cockneys came running through the door, faces alight in anticipation. You should have seen their faces when they saw me and big Stuart stood behind the bar, bare-chested.

Another quiet afternoon, when there was hardly anyone around, the front door slammed open and two armed police officers came running into the pub pointing their guns at me. Their faces were probably as surprised as mine. One of them said:

'Hello Steve, what are you doing here?'

I answered them with both my hands in the air. 'Working, why? What are you doing?'

It turned out that they were chasing a suspect in an armed robbery that had just occurred in a warehouse around the corner and they had lost him in the vicinity of the Mount Pleasant pub.

One night we were visited by a group of Chelsea fans who started to get a bit loud and boisterous. They ignored all our nice requests to calm down. Our locals soon vanished. I looked at Andy and big Stuart and then walked around from behind the bar to the front door. Thinking that they had us worried, the Chelsea lads were singing football songs, banging their glasses and being stupid. Football hooligans can usually have a good go, especially at the right time and place, but these lads had got a little bit complacent thinking that they had frightened us into submissive behaviour.

When I locked the door and Andy and Stuart came around from behind the bar, those Chelsea yobs finally realised that we weren't worried at all, we were just pissed off with them. By the time we had finished with them they were begging us to let them out of the place, in fact a couple of them even tried locking themselves in the ladies' toilets. Obviously not the right place or right time, eh?

20

Door War

THE SON OF my good friend Graham Blow was turning twenty-one and Graham invited my wife Tanee and me to a meal in a nice restaurant in a small town called Kirkham, just a few miles from Blackpool. The dinner went well with everybody enjoying themselves. My friend Steve Daley was there and also present were Simon McDougal, now sadly deceased, and Karl Etherington.

Simon was about twenty-six years old and a professional light-heavyweight boxer. Karl was about twenty-two at the time and a judo expert as well as being a good streetfighter. He later won the English heavyweight judo championship. Although they were good friends of mine, the pair of them could be a door firm's nightmare when they turned up at a club off their heads.

During the course of the meal, Simon and Karl told me a tale about the previous evening in Blackpool. They had visited Addison's nightclub in Talbot Square and had managed to get into a little bit of bother with the door staff. The way they told it, the door staff were out of order. You know what it's like, it's always the door staff's fault.

Anyway, a couple of hours later – after quite a few drinks – the four of us decided, in our infinite wisdom, like you do, to go into Blackpool and have a word with the manager of the club about the behaviour of his security.

The manager, Peter Rowland, was an old friend of mine from the Foxhall days. The door staff were employed by Northern Security, Steve Hill's firm.

The doormen did try to stop us from getting in but we were insistent. What we didn't know was that the police had given the club special instructions to phone them straight away if Karl and Simon showed up again. The doormen did ring the police but only after they had rung their boss, Steve Hill. It turned out that Steve Hill was a bit pissed off with Karl Etherington. Apparently he had been causing havoc at a lot of the clubs and pubs that Northern Security looked after. This could be payback time.

The four of us were inside Addison's on the top floor when Steve Hill and about twelve of his men, all dressed in black or navy blue suits, turned up looking eager for a confrontation. They certainly looked the part.

It kicked off big-style, with tables, chairs and even a cigarette machine being knocked over. I caught Steve Hill with a couple of head shots and thought, in my alcohol-induced state, that I was doing quite well until, bang, a big right cross landed on my chin and turned me upside down.

Shaking my head I got to my feet. Fuck me! That had sobered me up a bit. What the fuck were we doing facing these numbers here and now? The next thing I knew, someone had a half-nelson chokehold on me from behind and I couldn't breathe. Going down onto one knee, I heard this cunt whispering into my ear, 'You're not so hard now are you, you prick.'

I had to agree with him at that moment, as I was fading fast with the lack of oxygen. I could not speak, so I just tapped his arm. I couldn't believe it when he let me go. Taking a deep breath, I stood up and turned to face him. I had never seen him before but I wiped the smirk off of his face, along with some of his teeth. Luck was still on my side.

Once more into the breach, we will fight them on the beaches and all that crap. I went into the middle of it again. We struggled on until we came to a standstill, not a bad outcome considering the odds against us. As the four of us left, the police were just arriving at the club so we did a quick sidestep the other way.

The next morning Tanee woke me up and said, 'Some of your pals are outside waiting to see you.' Sarcastic cow, it was only the Cunts In Disguise (CID).

As soon as I opened the front door, they arrested me for 'assault on Stephen Hill'. I laughed at them and said, 'There is no way you will make that stick.' I knew Steve wouldn't press charges.

Steve Daley, Karl Etherington, Simon McDougal and I were all charged with numerous offences, from actual bodily harm to affray. This became the talk of the town in Blackpool and caused a large amount of unrest. I had a visit from a uniformed police officer warning me that the police were aware that there was a contract offering a substantial amount of money to kill Stephen Hill. I was also told that Mr Hill had been provided with an emergency alarm system that went straight to the police.

The daft cunts, we had already shaken hands over the incident.

I was also banned from entering any licensed premises in the country, which was a bit naughty seeing as how I was looking after a couple. The case was committed to Preston Crown Court. I bet you can't guess the judge? Yep! His Honour Judge Duckworth was sitting.

Oh fuck! I don't believe this, it must be a conspiracy.

If I say he tried to go to town on us, it could class as an understatement. Steve Hill did not want to give evidence and he had gone on holiday to Spain. When my favourite judge was informed of this he immediately adjourned the case and sent a message to Steve Hill, saying that if he was not in the courtroom by such a time on such a date he would be charged with trying to pervert the course of justice. Steve had to return but things did not go the prosecution's way, much to the judge's disgust.

The trial ended up with four different juries being sworn in over a period of a few weeks. None of us was sure of what was happening but in the end the case against us was dismissed because of all the adverse publicity in the north-west papers, such as 'Door Wars in Blackpool'. Our defence barristers had rightly argued that we were not doormen and that the news coverage had made it impossible for the fourth jury to be impartial or unaffected.

It just goes to show that some incidents can be taken out of context by the authorities. Everything would have been over with and forgotten months before at no cost to the public if they had left it to us, with the same outcome.

Shortly after all the commotion had died down, I was approached by Stephen Swallow, with whom I had been friendly since the night I was stabbed outside Just Ji's nightclub many years before. Steve now ran a successful company, Swallow Security, and he needed a right-hand man. He offered me the job on condition that the Blackpool chief of police did not object to my appointment. I thought he was taking the piss; there was no way the Old Bill would agree to this. Yet to my surprise they did, with only a couple of conditions concerning my future behaviour.

At the time, Swallow Security had contracts in Blackpool such as the Heaven and Hell nightclub, which held a couple of thousand revellers. This was the flagship club of a man named Peter Clarke, who was opening similar venues across the north-west of England. Steve also had the security contract for The Business, another large club that could hold a couple of thousand, and quite a few smaller venues. He also had static and retail sites. All in all, he was running a nice business.

When I started with Steve Swallow, it amazed me that he kept most of the information for the different jobs that he was covering in his head. As the company expanded, however, we started to use those new-fangled things called computers. Business went from strength to strength, with Swallow Security winning more and more local contracts and even coming in the top three in a national competition for small businesses. Every chance he got, Steve would show off the photographs of him down in London with the then-Chancellor, Gordon Brown. Mind you, it was something to be proud of.

Swallow Security took over the security for the Syndicate superclub on Church Street in Blackpool. The Syndicate is enormous: it holds up to four thousand people and if you average one doorman per one hundred customers, that means forty security staff. We managed to put quite a good team on there, run by Steve Powell. Steve was well known in the amateur boxing circles across the country, particularly as a referee, but sadly he passed away in 2007 of a heart attack.

One Saturday night, Steve Powell called my mobile phone and asked me to get there as quick as I could to give him some back-up.

'Back up?' I said. 'There's forty of you there, what fucking good is one more man going to do?'

When I arrived at the club, it turned out that there were two large teams of men facing off with each other. Some of our men were a little bit worried and were asking Steve Powell to get the police in to sort it out. Assessing the situation, I asked Steve what he wanted to do.

'I want to get them out,' he replied.

So that was what we did, and to be truthful it was a lot easier than we thought it would be. We focused all our strength on one team, took them straight out through the fire doors, then went back and did the same to the other team. If we had split up and tried to take them both out at the same time, we would have been caught in a three-way fight. Divide and conquer is the key, but that sort of knowledge only comes with experience on the doors.

I had also been looking after the door at the Blue night-club on Corporation Street, which was the new name for the old Promises club. There were three of us on the security team: Paul Kirby (later landlord at the Empress Hotel), David 'Dinger' Bell and me. It was a busy club before the Syndicate opened and many of the locals were attracted there.

There was never much trouble at Blue but a couple of times it did go off big time between me and a local face by the name of Peter Mason. His family had for years run the 'mock auctions', in which gullible punters would be enticed by promises of bargains only to end up with cheap tat. Peter, who I believe has been mentioned in a couple of books and also once featured on the *Cook Report* TV programme, was once acquitted of drugs offences after what was said to be the longest-running criminal trial in UK history. He was also on the British judo team some years back. His grappling skills were considerable and he was known as a man who could look after himself.

The first time we tangled was when he was having an argument with a lad I knew and I intervened. As I butted him, he took me down with him, very slick and very impressive. I finally managed to pin him down by his throat but only after I had sustained a dislocated elbow. The second time we tangled, he bit a chunk from my face when I had hold of him, and his nancy pal Steve Leahy hit me over the head with a bottle from behind. The last time we tangled, I destroyed him with one punch. Mind you, it was a fucking great punch.

Peter had turned up at the club with a strong firm, including a big gypsy bareknuckle fighter by the name of Jervace and half a dozen other men. He had pushed past Dave Bell and the other lad normally on duty, Paul Kirby, wasn't working that night. By the time I had spotted them they had bought a round of drinks.

At the time I was talking to Barry Singleton. Now

Barry could do a bit and he was always up for a fight if it was forced upon him. Asking him to watch my back, I walked over to the group and told Peter he was not welcome and he would have to leave. He was actually quite civil when he spoke.

'I have just bought a round of drinks.'

'As soon as you have finished them, then. Okay?' I replied.

I walked back to Barry thinking to myself, *that went well.*

As the group finished their drinks, they headed for the door. Peter turned and looked my way. I could see it coming. He shook his head and came my way.

I knew it had been too easy.

He started talking, being calm and logical at first but when I wouldn't let them stay he soon changed his tune: 'Look at who you are dealing with, look how outnumbered you are ...'

The big gypsy lad was brand new, he kept saying to Peter, 'The man is just doing his job, let's go.'

But Peter wouldn't listen. In the end he said to me, 'If you want me out you will have to throw me out.'

Well my arse was twitching, I can promise you that. I looked at him and just let loose, one punch that travelled from my thigh up through his chin; not to his chin, through it. I nearly took the top of his head off.

The big man shook my hand and dragged Mason out by his ankle. Top man Jervace. About fifteen minutes later, the police turned up at the front door of the club asking for me. I couldn't believe it. Walking down the stairs I could see two uniforms, one an inspector and the other a sergeant. They both looked at me as I stopped in front of them.

The inspector stared me in the eye and said, 'Steve, we have just seen Peter Mason outside. Are you responsible for the condition he is in?'

When I said yes, they both shook my hand.

The security industry was undergoing a massive change. Every single person working in the industry would need a licence; not the local council licences that had been around for the past few years but nationally recognised ones that required each applicant to undergo stringent training in the rules and procedures for security staff and conflict management. The police and local councils had been responsible for the training of door supervisors in the past but now it was to be a national Level 2 award (in education a Level 2 is equivalent to a GCSE).

The local licensing police officer contacted Northern Security and Swallow Security and asked if we would be willing to take over the task of training between us. Although there had been a lot of bad history between Swallow Security and Northern Security, and between Stephen Hill and me, Tommy Baldwin and I had always got on with each other. Tommy, who is also an ex-boxer, is Steve Hill's right-hand man. It was agreed that Tommy Baldwin from Northern Security and myself from Swallow Security would step up to the challenge.

That was when they informed us that whoever accepted the task would need to acquire a recognised training or teaching qualification. It meant two years at Blackpool College studying for a Professional Certificate in Education. Tommy was not too bothered about this, as he already held a Bachelor of Arts degree with honours. But my record in education so far had been patchy, to say the least.

For the first few weeks it was like they were talking a different language in the classroom, but slowly it all started to sink in and make sense. There was a group of four of us that sat together in the corner of the room: Tommy, Fez (a physical training instructor from Kirkham open prison), Barry (a disc jockey better known as Funky

B) and me. The tutors called it the naughty corner. It is funny how four grown men can revert to schoolboy mentality even though they all come from different backgrounds. So I would like to thank Debbie Swift and Vincent Farrell, our teacher training tutors at the Blackpool and Fylde College, for all their help and guidance – and for putting up with us.

I was with Swallow Security for about six years and everything was going very well until an accountant ended up having the firm bang over. He had allegedly been transferring monies into his accounts instead of paying taxes. The company ended up having to go into receivership and even though Steve transferred his undertakings he could no longer be the managing director of the firm. His son Anthony stepped up to that position and Steve took over my job, which in effect made me redundant. I honestly don't understand why that accountant is still walking around but what the heck, that's down to Swallow.

Luckily for me – as this occurred just a few weeks before Christmas in 2004, not a great time to lose your job – I was offered a higher-paid position by Northern Security the same day that I found out I was being made redundant.

I graduated on July 5, 2005, the first person in my immediate family to earn any type of degree. (My eldest daughter Kelly is now also getting ready to graduate herself from the Blackpool and the Fylde College; she will receive a Bachelor of Arts in Hospitality Management. I am very proud of her.)

Tommy and I were both offered what are known as fractional positions, teaching security courses for the college. Although the police seemed to be happy to leave me alone, I kept receiving information that people who were being pulled in over alleged involvement in serious crimes were being asked questions about me. A close friend of mine who witnessed a crime was shown the mugshot book to see if she could identify any suspects. Leafing through pages full of dubious characters, she was very surprised to find a picture of me. She was not as surprised as I was when she told me about it.

Imagine my shock when the enhanced Criminal Record Bureau check that I needed to work for Blackpool College came back. I had needed a normal CRB check for my Security Industry Authority licence and that came back clean. The enhanced report was clean too but the comments by the chief of police on the back referred to 'Information held linking Stephen Sinclair to organised crime' between certain dates.

I was gobsmacked. I went to a solicitor and asked him to find out what was happening. How the fuck can they get away with something like that? I had never been convicted or even questioned about any such allegations. The College were confused as to what course of action they should take regarding my continuing employment with them. I could not blame them really.

In the end things just carried on as they were. Tommy Baldwin and I successfully trained approximately one thousand door supervisors through the Blackpool and Fylde College. Since then we have trained a further one thousand or so for alert security training.

The second part of the National Certificate for Door Supervisors course is the conflict management unit. Conflict management is about recognising and defusing conflict without using force. The first time that we actually ran the course, we had an audience at the back of the room, consisting of a couple of uniformed police officers. When I approached them to ask why they were there, one of them replied, smiling, 'We just had to come, we wanted to see Steve Sinclair teaching people how not to fight.' The cheeky bastards.

In 2006, I was approached by the producer of the television journalist Donal McIntyre's programmes to see if I would be interested in being involved in his series on the criminal underworld, portraying Blackpool. I grace-fully declined, wishing to let sleeping dogs lie. I have now retired from the frontline doors; at least I hope so. I do still occasionally look after my good friend Paul Kirby's place, the Empress Hotel in North Shore, when he needs me, but other than that, and seeing that I was fifty years old on August 13, 2007, I think enough is enough.

Saying that, it was only a few months ago that I was sat with Paul having a quiet drink after an evening shift when a brick came flying through the hotel window. Rushing outside, I was confronted by a man holding a big boxer dog on a lead and a bat. I looked at them and thought to myself, I am either going to get beaten with a bat or bitten by a dog. Oh well. I ended up taking the bat from the guy and hitting him with it. You may ask what happened to the dog. Well that big lovable boxer that he obviously thought would act as a deterrent ended up biting him. Good boy!

Mind you, I have still found myself on the doors for Northern Security in Salford (Swinton) and Liverpool (Bootle) if we are short of staff when a new Yates's venue is opened or they are having serious trouble with the locals.

Blackpool is full of characters that have come from all over the world. Some of them are trying to make it their home while others are just trying to make a few pounds before moving on elsewhere. Either way, please remember that if you come to Blackpool to enjoy yourself, the locals will accommodate and try to make sure you have a good time. If you come to Blackpool looking for trouble, they will still try to accommodate you but in a very different way.

Doormen are not always the most popular of charac-ters. Some of them have a reputation for mindless thuggery, not all of it undeserved. But in a place like Blackpool, they do a thankless job. It would be impossible for any book to list the sheer number of violent incidents that take place in the town in a year, never mind a lifetime. Here is just one fairly recent story, from the local *Evening Gazette*, that shows the kind of situation the doormen have to deal with to protect their customers:

A gang of bikers armed with knives, knuckle-dusters and CS gas waged running battles in a terrifying eruption of violence.

A gang of up to 25 brawlers, claiming to belong to the Outlaws Motorcycle Club, put four people in hospital as a massive street brawl broke out in the early hours of yesterday.

At around 1am, Market Street, in central Blackpool, was transformed from a party area with numerous bars and clubs into a scene of horror.

The out-of-town bikers clashed with door supervisors from NTK nightclub. It is thought the Outlaws, who have chapters up and down the country and have links with the US-based Hells Angels, fought a pitched battle in the club after being denied entry.

David Daly, manager of Cahoots, sent two of his doorstaff to help their colleagues.

He said: 'It was a nasty scene. We had to stop people going out into the street for their own safety because of what was out there. Police turned up, but the group seemed to have no respect for them at all and took them on. There were people lying on the ground all over the place. My doormen went to help their colleagues at NTK and two of them were put in hospital.

'It was a real mess when the police arrived – a fight on the scale you just don't see any more. There was a time when you would see fights like this in the town – but not any more. They were kitted out in full gear. Leather biking trousers, big boots and waistcoats. When the police came there was a stand-off like in the movies with officers on one side and all these bikers in black on the other.'

Mike Sugden, manager at NTK, said all the doorstaff were excellent in keeping customers and staff safe.

Three doormen ended up being taken to hospital by paramedics after that incident. None of them were 'names', just £9-an-hour lads but they still did a job against a big, hard, tooled-up crew of proper blokes, not kids. And if I trawled through the archives of our local paper, I could find you scores of stories like that. It's not a job for the faint-hearted, not if you are going to do it properly.

I am still happily married to Tanee. Christie, my youngest daughter, has just started college. My grand-daughters are lovely girls. Peter Juggins is the owner land-lord of a beautiful public house just outside Winchester. Mark Wood has settled down to a quiet life somewhere in Southsea. My good friend Ian Sharples has moved from Blackpool to nearby Garstang and is very happy with Tracey and Emily, although he has hinted that when this book is published he might have to move further afield. Stephen Swallow runs Portal Security Services in Blackpool. Steve Hill still runs one of the biggest secu-rity firms in the north-west. Steve Warton has made a remarkable recovery from a brain haemorrhage.

My mate from Sheffield, Andy Trotter, has just phoned me to say he is 'looking at a big pub that's for sale, not far from Blackpool'.

Oh no!

BEFORE I FINALLY finish pressing these bloody computer keys, lots of people have asked me if I have ever killed anyone.

Another bit of very good advice that my old man gave me: if they weren't there, don't tell them anything.

You weren't there.

I hope you have enjoyed my story.